REA

Letters
from
Fort Lewis
Brig

Letters from Fort Lewis Brig

A Matter of Conscience

Kevin Benderman
with Monica Benderman

The Lyons Press
Guilford, Connecticut
An imprint of The Globe Pequot Press

The Lyons Press is an imprint of The Globe Pequot Press.

10 9 8 7 6 5 4 3 2 1

Printed in the United States of America

Designed by Diane Gleba Hall

ISBN 978-1-59228-933-2

Library of Congress Cataloging-in-Publication Data is available on file.

Contents

Preface

Statement of Monica Benderman on behalf of Sergeant Kevin Benderman

Congressional Briefing for Conscientious Objection
U.S. House of Representatives
Longworth House Office Building
Washington, DC
May 16, 2006

Thank you for giving me this time today. I would like to preface my comments to congressional representatives by reading a statement from my husband, Kevin Benderman, a U.S. Army sergeant who is currently serving a fifteen-month sentence at the Regional Corrections Facility, Fort Lewis, Washington.

From Kevin

I have prepared this statement to address the injustice I have been dealt by the U.S. Army after I made the decision to apply for conscientious objector status. I made this decision after my return from Iraq where I witnessed and experienced for myself the insanity of war.

What I learned from my experience is that war is a waste of humanity. We kill many people in the name of keeping the peace—an oxymoron if there ever was one. After many months of contemplation I reached the conclusion that I no longer wanted to contribute to the ultimate violence toward other human beings that war is.

I attempted to discuss my feelings with a chaplain assigned to my military unit, but I got the sense that talking with him would be a less than worthwhile way to cope with these feelings. Ultimately, my initial impression of him proved correct when I received an e-mail from him stating how ashamed of me he felt, and that I had displayed little moral fortitude in my decision.

The command structure of my unit was hostile toward me in its zealous need to have me prosecuted for having developed a desire to live a more peaceful, humane existence. I was ridiculed publicly, called a coward, subjected to a farce of a general court-martial, and falsely imprisoned.

The company commander refused to follow military regulations in regard to my conscientious objector application, and the battalion commander blatantly disregarded a request from a congressional representative to examine my application in an unbiased manner.

The general court-martial convening authority blatantly abused his position of authority when he told the Fort Stewart JAG [Judge Advocate General] office and the prosecuting attorneys how long my sentence would be prior to an investigation into charges they were considering against me. This action is a flagrant violation of my right to a fair and unbiased hearing accorded me by the Uniform Code of Military Justice.

The rear detachment commander also tried to dredge up any other groundless charges to press against me that he could. Two charges of larceny were brought in to try to further tarnish my reputation, which eventually proved groundless, but not before they were used as a threat to encourage me to plead guilty to an act I did not commit.

It is my desire to prevent other soldiers from having to deal with corrupt and unethical individuals like these commanders. I would like to see legislation passed that would prevent any type of abuses from those serving in positions of authority within the military system. The people who voluntarily decide to wear this nation's uniform already sacrifice far more than the average citizen. Their basic civil rights should not be sacrificed as well to the unethical whims of corrupt individuals who may hold a higher rank, but exhibit far less humanity. Any assistance in rectifying this situation would be greatly appreciated, and I would like to thank those who made it possible for me to present my remarks here today. I would also like to thank those of you who have taken time to hear what I have had to say.

Sincerely,

Sergeant Kevin Benderman

I will address my comments to the members of Congress: each one of you is in office having been elected on the basis of promises you made. In taking that office, each one of you took an oath to honor the Constitution of this country, and you did so by swearing to your God.

An American soldier, a volunteer, takes the same oath. His commitment to that oath is based on the promises of our elected leaders. But a true leader is not someone who blindly follows laws written by men. A true leader is someone who leads with adherence to his own obligation to humanity. If you, during your tenure and contract to serve as congressional leaders, were asked to participate in an action that violated your own conscience and your own principles of humanity, would you take a stand against that action?

If you were to step down, no longer willing to participate in an immoral, illegal action, would you have charges brought against you?

Would you be sent to jail for your beliefs? Would you go willingly? Would you allow this to happen to any member who serves with you, who also acted on their conscience?

As a volunteer, an American soldier has every right to question the purpose of his sacrifice, and to expect that sacrifice to be honored with integrity and honesty, and to be allowed to follow his conscience when orders given violate his own principles of humanity.

Freedom of choice is one of the most significant principles on which our country was founded. Conscientious objection is the true exercise of a soldier's right to choose.

Do you understand what it takes to publicly declare yourself a conscientious objector today?

Are you aware of the process an American soldier must go through to be granted conscientious objector status in today's volunteer army?

My husband, Sergeant Kevin Benderman, is a ten-year veteran of the U.S. Army and has served with distinction. He served a combat tour in Iraq and was awarded two Commendation Medals for his service there. While in Iraq, my husband's firsthand experiences changed him.

My husband went to war. He saw mass graves filled with dead bodies of old people, women, and children. He watched dogs feeding on their bodies. How would that affect you?

He saw a young girl badly burned because of the actions of war and rather than stop to help her, war dictated that he must drive on by. How would that tear at your heart?

As he helped set up camp, his commander gave his unit an order to shoot small children if they continued to return to the top of a retaining wall to watch what the soldiers were doing. At what point would you draw the line?

What he saw and experienced appalled him, and he was angry. My husband left Iraq cold and furious at what he had been asked to do for an unjust, undefined cause, and a dedicated soldier turned against war for moral and ethical reasons as his conscience would not allow him to violate his own principles of humanity.

When he returned home, my husband and I wrote publicly about our feelings for this and all war. We spoke of the horrors, the senseless inhumanity, and the disrespect shown to the sacrifice our soldiers had made.

My husband took the course available to him and filed a conscientious objector application as his legal show of refusal to participate further in an immoral, inhumane action.

His command, in an effort to punish him for his humanity, and because they could not do so for the public comments that he and I had made, chose to disregard his application, and in the confusion, their incompetence found a way to put him in prison for his actions.

Kevin was found guilty of missing movement—or not getting on a plane—and sentenced to fifteen months in jail, loss of all pay, reduction in rank, and dishonorable discharge. According to the lead prosecutor, the military spokesperson, and my husband's commander, "a stiff sentence was called for to send a message to other soldiers that they could not use conscientious objection to get out of going to war."

My husband violated no regulations. His command violated many. The command's flagrant disregard for military regulations and laws of humanity sent my husband to jail as a prisoner of conscience.

Times have changed—and so has conscientious objection. What has not changed is the Constitution, the oath our volunteer soldiers take to defend it, and every American citizen's right to freedom of choice.

This conscientious objection goes beyond religious teaching. It is not dramatic. There is no epiphany. There is reality. Death is final, whether it is your own or you cause the death of another. No amount of field training can make up for the sights, sounds, tastes, and smells of a real battlefield, and no amount of threats, intimidation, and abuse from a command can change a soldier's mind when the cold, hard truth of an immoral, unethical justification for war is coupled with real-life sensations.

Who among us has the authority to sit in judgment of another man's conscious decision to no longer participate in killing, when he has been on the front lines of death and destruction?

Simply by being born we each have an obligation to respect the authority of *life*, as individual human beings with an allegiance to what is right, not an allegiance to a flag, a country, or another human being elected to a temporary position of leadership they may not have earned.

When a soldier realizes that his conscience no longer supports the oath he gave to serve in the military, it is because he has learned that what he was asked to do as a soldier violates his obligation to himself and his humanity.

My husband was scheduled for a parole hearing in February 2006. The parole board denied my husband's request for parole. The reason cited: my husband had not been "sufficiently rehabilitated." My husband is a conscientious objector. What is the rehabilitation needed for someone who says he no longer will participate in war?

The right to choose life over the taking of life is every man's right. Regardless if that man has volunteered to defend his country in time of war, he did not volunteer to participate in wanton, irreverent killing at the whim of a government whose leadership is quick to "pull the trigger" without giving thought to the authority of the sanctity of life.

A true American leader will stand up to laws and orders given that violate the sanctity of life and call the principles of our Constitution into question. A true American leader will let his conscience be his guide when asked to participate in actions that violate his own high standards of morality. When this leader is a soldier who has made a choice to stand against the inhumanity he has seen firsthand in a combat zone, it is up to those in Congress to see that laws are in place that give his right to conscience the respect it deserves.

I am here on behalf of my husband, Sergeant Kevin Benderman: American soldier, prisoner of conscience, someone I am very proud of.

My husband and others like him are in prison because our country's leaders have refused to acknowledge their responsibility to act as human beings first. My husband, a volunteer soldier, after a combat tour in Iraq, chose to put his humanity first. It is beyond my comprehension why, in this great country, my husband is in jail simply for exercising his human rights.

It is time for each of you to remember your obligation to humanity and act in a manner that is truly worthy of my husband's sacrifice. I am strongly encouraging each of you to reflect on your responsibility and your conscience, and in doing so, I am advocating that my husband, Sergeant Kevin Benderman, be given the respect he deserves as a conscientious objector and an American leader who has taken a stand to defend the principles this country was founded on.

Introduction

There comes a time in your life when you have to reexamine the course you have set for yourself in order to determine if it is still the best one to take. I actively served as a U.S. Army soldier for about ten years, with four years' individual ready reserve time (this is a component of the service for those not on active duty), but after my experience with war and the devastation it brings to people, I found myself at a crossroads: Do I continue to pursue the path of a career soldier, or do I make the change to become a different person?

Should I continue to be someone who would not hesitate to go to war and kill other human beings for imaginary reasons? Should I make the changes that we all should and start using reason and thought to reach sound resolutions in order to be able to live with the differences between ourselves and others?

The decision would be very complex, and the answer would not come easily. There were many factors to consider as I faced the decision I had to make. The biggest was the fact that my army buddies would feel as if I were letting them down, and the next was the fact that members of my family have participated in the armed services of this country from the American Revolution up until today. I would be breaking the tradition that many generations, from both my mother's and father's side of the family, had established since then.

I was raised in the South, where there is a very strong sense of pride if you are in the armed services. Civil War memorials are everywhere, and it is the underlying atmosphere that to serve in the military sets you apart from the average man. I hope I have laid out clearly some of the factors that influenced my decision to serve.

Some people feel the only reason that anyone serves in the military is for the educational benefits, commissary privileges, and/or the medical benefits. I cannot deny the reality of people needing those things to provide for their family, but there are much deeper reasons to serve than just the superficial ones like money and benefits. In the cynical world we live in, many of us will not believe that someone can serve in the military for anything other than the financial benefits. But the fact is, many in the military truly serve out of a sense of "duty, honor, and country." In fact, I would say the majority of the people in the armed services are there because of those very reasons and not because they are the dregs of society who cannot do anything else. Far too many people in the civilian world try to put that stigma on the service members and, unfortunately, this is the image of military personnel they want to hold on to.

People in the military have to be dedicated, because the pay isn't really that great. Most people seem to believe that soldiers are rolling in dough, but that isn't the case. In 1987 when I first enlisted as an E-1—a private, the lowest rank possible—the starting salary was a whopping $650 per month. When I reenlisted in 2000, the starting pay was $1,100 per month for an E-1 private. I really do not understand why people think that soldiers are making out like fat cats, because that is far from reality. You need to factor in all of the everyday things that soldiers miss out on that most folks take for granted, like the baby's first steps, graduations, anniversaries, weddings, deaths in the family, and many more things that the average civilian never has to miss.

So if service members are getting a little bit more of a tax break than the average civilian and they get a little free medical care (which isn't always that great), then they have earned it, because they put up with stuff the average American doesn't even contemplate, much less have to deal with. The next time you feel as if the service members were making too much money, try walking a mile in their boots.

Getting back to my original subject, making the decision to stop being a soldier and change my way of living to a more humane style was a very hard change to make. As I said, the influences were many that led me to become a soldier in the first place, so the decision to leave it all behind was more difficult than people will ever know. Some people are confused over how I could do so without consulting everyone and talking to everyone about my decision. I have to say that I talked with the people who matter to me most, which are the members of my family.

I don't really care if people do not understand how I can keep the decision that affects only my family a private matter. In this day and age when everyone gets on TV and spouts all of their most private information for the whole world to hear, I think it amazes people that I kept this a private family matter. If it weren't for the individuals in my unit who forced my hand, it would have remained a private family matter. I had spent many months going over this situation in my head. I had many discussions with my wife, Monica, about the best path to take. I had attempted to talk with the battalion chaplain about this for months, and he would always find a reason to put me off. After I had filed the application for conscientious objector status, he sent me an e-mail saying that he was ashamed of me for doing so.

In order to explain a little more clearly my decisions to serve and then to declare myself a conscientious objector, I think I need to go back to my childhood. I was a typical southern boy, and by that I mean I spent more time outside the house than in. My brother and I did all the things you would expect of two boys in the South: We spent many a day at a creek, fishing with homemade poles and camping out with two of our friends from down the road. When I say "down the road," I mean about five miles away. Anyway, we would put our stuff in a wagon and then we would head out to a halfway point between our house and theirs, where we would go into a grassy area surrounded by trees. We would build a fire in a pit that we made with the bricks and the grate we had scrounged, and then we would grill the hot dogs we had bought after we had collected enough empty bottles of "Coke-cola" (every type of soft drink was called Coke-cola where I come from) from the ditch to take back to the store to redeem the deposit so we could pay for them.

I remember always being very interested in seeing the National Guard soldiers doing their weekend training as they would go by in their convoys of big army trucks. (I now know them to be the fabled 2.5-ton truck, better known as the "deuce and a half," but back then they were just big army trucks.) I would always imagine that it was me up there driving that big truck. We also had those green plastic army men, the trucks that came with them, and the little tanks. My brother and I would fight the most terrible battles from the big wars right there in our backyard. We would use leftover fireworks from the Fourth of July as the bombs and grenades that would blow the little plastic army men in every direction of the compass. When it was all over, we would do it again.

As we got a little older, we both had BB guns, and we would wage mock battles in the backyard as cowboys and Indians. We would shoot each other with the BBs, the only rule being that we could not shoot each other in the head; everything else from the shoulders on down was open game. As we grew and started making friends of our own, we began hanging around them more. I cannot speak for my brother, but I can say for myself that the imaginary wars continued up until I was about fourteen or so, when more important things started getting my attention (that is an entirely different story). The friends I had at the time thought it was great to go to the woods and build forts out of sticks and pine straw. We would wage mock wars from these things as well. Pinecones make great imitation hand grenades, and let me tell you, when they are green, they hurt pretty badly when you are hit with one.

After that I guess I went through that stage that all teens go through—I thought I knew it all, and you could not tell me a thing. I couldn't care less about authority figures. Not that I was that bad of a young person, I guess. It was just that no one knew more than I did, and I was going to let everyone know it. In those dim, dark days of my youth, people weren't quite as attentive to age limits on drinking as they are now, and I exploited it every chance I got. A few of my buddies and I would go to the liquor store and get some beer or whis-key when we had the money. We would proceed to get falling-down drunk until we got ourselves sick. Afterward, we would recover and do it all over again.

I remember being approached by two navy recruiters at the pool-room arcade where I spent a lot of time. They were trying to get me to join the navy, and I laughed at them and told them there was no way. I was eighteen at the time that happened, and you could not tell me a thing, because I owned the world. Looking back on that time, I felt that at eighteen years old I was not mature enough to handle the responsibility of being in the military. About four years later, I was starting to change my thinking a little and was becoming more inter-ested in the history of my family's service to the country. The more I thought about it, the better the concept sounded, so I went to talk to the army recruiter in Decatur, Alabama. I enlisted then for the first time. I was twenty-two years old, and I still thought I knew a lot. But I realized by then that I did not know it all.

My first enlistment was from January 27, 1987, until April 30, 1991, and the Military Occupational Specialty I enlisted for was 91R, Veteri-nary Food Inspection Specialist. I went to basic training at Fort Bliss, Texas, and boy, let me say, it was everything I thought it would be, and it was different from what I thought as well, if that makes any sense. After basic and advanced individual training, I was stationed at Fort Leavenworth, Kansas. This was a rather uneventful place to be until the Persian Gulf War. There were some interesting things happening there, though. I remember seeing some foreign soldiers attending the Command and General Staff College (CGSC). The soldiers were offi-cers from Iraq, and they were taking classes at the CGSC and the War College, both of which are located at Fort Leavenworth. The schools are designed to train our officers in war-fighting tactics and techniques using the lessons learned in previous wars. I thought nothing of it at the time, but when we went to war against Iraq in 1990, I looked back to 1988 and remember thinking to myself how odd this was—to be training the officers of the Iraqi Army and then to be fighting them not two years later.

I remember the feelings I had about the war at that time. I was a little nervous about the prospect of war, but I was able to control my fear, and I was fully prepared to go and do what I had to do. The unit I was in went through all of the preparations to go to Iraq; half the unit had already been sent, and the other half was getting ready to go when the war was declared over—the objective had been met. I was a little disgusted at the time about how the war was conducted because I felt that if we were going to lose soldiers in order to free Kuwait, then we should have gone all the way to Baghdad to take out the leaders of the country that had started all the trouble in the first place.

By this time I was disgusted with how the military was generally operated. One of the reasons I felt that way was the fact that my supervisor was being run out of the army by the very people who were claiming to look out for soldiers like him. At the time, he had served for almost seventeen years. The guy wasn't the most high-speed or gung-ho soldier out there, but he had served solidly. The reason for his trouble with the army was because he started having problems with his wife who was asking him for a divorce. The guy became depressed and started drinking more than he should, and instead of getting him help (the unit preached about how they always looked out for soldiers), the senior enlisted man of the section where I worked went after this guy and was dead set on burning him. Well, eventually the noncommissioned officer in charge (NCOIC) was successful, and the guy was kicked out of the army and lost all the benefits he had worked for. That was when I started to get bad feelings for what the army really was like underneath the surface glitter.

They talk a good game about looking out for soldiers, but when the chips are down, they really don't give a shit about you. This isn't the only example of this type of thing, either. Another man who was serving at the time had nearly nineteen years in, and his knee was starting to give him trouble from all of the running he had done over the years. Instead of letting him finish out his time in an administrative position, the commander of the unit tried to get him out on an unfit-for-duty discharge, which would have cost him all his retirement benefits.

So, I decided to get out of the army and did so in April of 1991 after the Persian Gulf War. I decided to go back to doing what I had learned to do prior to my initial enlistment, which was floor-covering installation. This is a good trade in which you can make good money, but it is very hard work. I bought a van and the initial tools needed to start working for myself, and I proceeded to work as an independent contractor.

Doing this type of work once again was challenging, and the money I made was pretty good, but there was always a nagging feeling that I had left something unfinished. I had started talking to my father about being in the army, because he had fought in World War II. He told me that I should not go back into the army because I was not the type of person who should be in the military. I never had a father-knows-best type of relationship with my dad, so I listened to what he had to say and then promptly ignored his advice. I should have really listened to him, because he was right.

My dad served in the army during World War II, and I guess he had seen some pretty rough stuff while he was in France and Belgium. He had a Purple Heart for wounds received while fighting in France. He never told us war stories when we were young. As a matter of fact, he never talked much about his experience with war until I was in the army. My father started opening up, and he related a story about a soldier he saw walking along a road, heading to the aid station. He was surprised that the soldier was walking, as he had been shot in the stomach; somehow, he was still able to make his way by himself.

He told me another story about the lieutenant who had been put in charge of the bazooka team that he was part of. The lieutenant wanted to set the team in a place where my dad had seen some German soldiers recently, and my dad thought they would be coming back to the same spot. He tried to tell the lieutenant what he thought was about to happen, but the lieutenant would not listen. My dad said that he was not going to stay in that area and moved across the road to a more secure location with some of the members of the team. He said about twenty minutes later the enemy soldiers came back to the spot they had left earlier, attacked the rest of the team, and killed them and the lieutenant. My father received shrapnel wounds from the ensuing firefight, for which he received the Purple Heart.

My point in telling this story is to say that all war is the same, whether it is World War I or II, Korea, Vietnam, Desert Storm, Panama, Bosnia, Operation Iraqi Freedom, or any other conflict that has ever been fought. War is the most brutal way to get your point across, and

I believe that we can do much better than this. We have been at war almost constantly since we have been on the planet, and what has it really accomplished?

My own experience with war is what led to my filing for conscientious objector status. What I saw and learned about it made me realize that war really solves nothing. It just turns our young men and women into people we would never teach them to be. I went to Iraq not with stars in my eyes because I was older, and I realized that war is not the glorious and glamorous thing the movies make it out to be. I did go because I was told that we were protecting our home from the terrible terrorists who were out to get us all. I was sold a bill of goods, and I bought it.

Some of the experiences that I had led me to change my mind about war as a solution to the problems we face. I was told to shoot children who were doing nothing more than being children. There were mass graves all over the place. I also met people who were no different from people I knew at home; there are engineers in Iraq, construction workers, plumbers, mechanics, and many others who are very similar to my friends and family. I could no longer, in good conscience, take part in the thing I realized was a waste of time, a waste of our resources, and a waste of our most valuable commodity—our young people.

Another reason for my decision was the effect this madness was having on my family. Monica was having a hard time with my being in the line of fire in a war zone, and it was hard to watch her go through the emotional turmoil she was experiencing. I did not want to know that I might cause her to stand at my graveside to watch them put the dirt on my coffin.

There was also my mother to think of, as she was getting older, and I did not want to put her through that emotional trauma either. It is really hard to put all these feelings into words for the entire world to read, but I feel it's important to explain the reasons I have for declaring myself a conscientious objector to war.

War in America is glamorized entirely too much, and I know the truth about it. It is not glorious. It is not a way to become a man. It is nothing but a destroyer of all that is good about our world. It makes you become a cold-blooded killer. You have to put all of your emotions away in order to survive. It forces our young people to become mindless automatons in order to make it home alive.

The movies play a big role in making war seem like it is a great thing, and it is irresponsible for the movie studios to do this. *Rambo* is a very good example. The first installment attempts to tell the story of what the Vietnam veterans were feeling as they returned home from war and had to deal with their emotions. This is not necessarily bad, but the subsequent movies about Rambo were played up to make war seem like it is cool or that it makes you a man.

This is just one example of how movies use the concept of war to make huge profits and to subsequently portray war as something great and glorious. We need to change how we portray war in our pop media culture, because the reality of war is 180 degrees different from what is shown on television and at the movies.

Sergeant Kevin Benderman
Conscientious Objector
November 2006

DEPARTMENT OF THE ARMY

THIS IS TO CERTIFY THAT THE SECRETARY OF THE ARMY HAS AWARDED

THE ARMY COMMENDATION MEDAL

TO

SERGEANT KEVIN M. BENDERMAN
C TROOP, 1ST SQUADRON, 10TH U.S. CAVALRY REGIMENT

FOR MERITORIOUS SERVICE WHILE ASSIGNED AS A SENIOR M3A3 BRADLEY MECHANIC. SGT
BENDERMAN'S DEDICATION AND TECHNICAL EXPERTISE HAVE BEEN VITAL TO THE SUCCESS OF
THE SQUADRON. HIS TIRELESS EFFORTS REFLECT GREAT CREDIT UPON HIMSELF, THE FOURTH
INFANTRY DIVISION, AND THE UNITED STATES ARMY.

FROM 14 MARCH 2001 TO 30 OCTOBER 2003

GIVEN UNDER MY HAND IN THE CITY OF WASHINGTON
THIS 20TH DAY OF AUGUST 2003

PERMANENT ORDER# 232-15

MICHAEL E. MOODY
COL, AV
Commanding

HEADQUARTERS, FOURTH BRIGADE
4TH INFANTRY DIVISION
TIKRIT, IRAQ, APO AE 09323

DA FORM 4980-14, NOV 97

Kevin's Army Commendation Medal certificate for meritorious service
from March 2001 through October, 2003.

Kevin leaving court and heading to prison after his court-martial on
July 28, 2005, at Fort Stewart, Georgia.

1: Preparing for Iraq

February 2002

Kevin We met. Meeting Monica was a big improvement in my otherwise mundane existence. It was never boring after that. I was going to see her when I had the extra time, and she came to see me when she could (which wasn't as often as I would have liked). Spending time with her was very good, but it went by too fast.

Monica There were five hours of travel between Fort Hood, which is just outside Killeen, Texas, where Kevin was stationed, and the small coastal town in southeastern Texas where I lived. We spent many evening hours on the telephone talking and even more hours sending e-mails and instant messages. We talked of everything imaginable and then some.

Kevin was serving in the 1st Squadron, 10th Cavalry Regiment of the 4th Infantry Division. We didn't talk much from mid-March to the end of April, as his unit was sent to the National Training Center (NTC) at Fort Irwin, California. When he returned, Kevin was already warning me that it looked as if they were preparing to invade Iraq. Almost every time we talked, he would make some mention of the possibility, and even without much prior experience with having a personal relationship with a soldier, I could sense that he was preparing me for what he had come to believe was inevitable.

Kevin I thought it odd at the time that there was so much talk about going to Iraq. It felt crazy to be getting ready for war with that country, because I thought they had nothing to do with the September 11 attacks on our nation. Now all of the evidence shows there was no connection between Saddam Hussein and Osama bin Laden.

June 2002

Monica Kevin was sent for a month of training in the army's Primary Leadership Development Course, and another month went by with virtually no conversation except the two phone calls he managed to make during his limited time off.

He completed the course and graduated at the top of his class, sergeant major out of four hundred soldiers. After graduation, things returned to what had become normal as far as communications and conversations. It wasn't long before he felt that he would be able to have some leave time to come for a visit. At this point, an invasion of Iraq seemed even more probable, and we wanted to take the time we had to become better acquainted before there was no time left.

August 2002

Monica Kevin came to visit me at work. At the time, I was working as care director for an assisted-living facility. The residents were wonderful people; at times I felt as if I had one hundred grandparents and loved them all. They were excited that Kevin was coming to visit. Many of the residents were survivors of World War II in some manner, either as the spouse of someone who had served or as a veteran. They respected that Kevin was a soldier, and the more we talked about Kevin and what he was doing, the more they opened up and reminisced about their own wartime experiences. Many were saddened to hear that there was talk of a possible invasion in Iraq. They remembered their war with mixed emotions, but almost every man who had served remembered hoping that there would never be another war. They talked about the attacks on the World Trade Center and the need to find those who had committed the hateful acts and bring them to justice. But in the very same conversations, they expressed their deep desire that it be done without war.

Kevin Talking with some of those veterans where Monica worked was very interesting, because they had the most amazing stories to tell about their experiences. Another thing I find rather unique about veterans is that no matter what era they served, there is a bond among them that you cannot find in any civilian occupation or endeavor. The World War II veterans treated me as though I had served directly with them. The same holds true for Korean and Vietnam veterans. Although I am from a different generation, we were all soldiers once.

Monica Kevin originally came to visit for the weekend, but after spending the time at the beach walking, talking, and just watching the waves, we found ourselves drawn to the conversations and each other's company, and the weekend extended to a week. Everything happens for a reason. This was a week well spent.

When Kevin left to return to Fort Hood, he let me know that it was becoming all the more evident his unit would be preparing to deploy to Iraq by the end of the year. He was preparing me for what was coming, and I knew he probably knew more than he could tell me.

October 2002

Monica Kevin reenlisted.

Kevin My sense of duty to country and the ideals our Constitution set forth were and are still very strong. That is why I decided to reenlist in October 2002. Much has been said about my reenlisting and then deciding to file for conscientious objector status. The people who orchestrated my courts-martial kept trying to say that I "re-upped" after I returned from Iraq, and that is why they wanted a harsh sentence. But they were sorely mistaken about the facts. The crazy thing to me about that is they keep on repeating erroneous information about my re-up date even though they know it is wrong.

Monica Kevin kept asking me, "Are you ready?" He seemed to know we'd eventually be together, even though I was a little more cautious. I was a civilian. Before Kevin, I had never had a close relationship with anyone in the military. His entire world was foreign to me. I had spent many years trying to get my life on track and to correct mistakes I had made by being too impetuous—thinking I could make everything go my way simply by attacking it all with reckless abandon. I had learned. There is a better way—and it is a way that brings peace. I had to be sure that everything I had learned would square with the feelings I was not sure I wanted to allow myself to have for a man who had made a decision to have a career as a soldier who fights wars.

Kevin I knew that we were meant to be together, so I would ask if she was ready for the long-term commitment that we were going to have. At first Monica thought I was joking around, but I knew what I knew, and I knew I wanted her to be my wife. I finally convinced her to see things my way, and we were married in February 2003, just before I deployed. Having a new wife and being sent to war was a two-sided coin: I was happy to be married, but I was leaving her to go to Iraq.

Monica In conversations, we would discuss the military and what life in the military meant. I was not naive—I knew what Kevin did. He made sure I knew that he had made a choice to make a career out of the military. He had plans to become a warrant officer—to work on the Bradley Fighting Vehicles and to teach others the same. He said he wasn't changing; it was who he was. I knew Kevin was a soldier. It was in his bearing. I thought a lot about what that meant. We were both strong, independent people who had gotten into many difficult situations in our lives because of our rebellious nature. We both knew what we wanted, and we didn't let anything interfere in finding ways to make it happen.

Kevin reenlisted to transfer to Fort Stewart, Georgia. His transfer was to take effect in the early spring of 2003 until he was ordered to remain with the 4th Infantry and deploy to Iraq under the military's stop-loss policy, which is designed to keep troops in service beyond their term. He would not move to Georgia until after he had redeployed at the end of his combat tour. This gave me more time to think through what I wanted and what it would mean, which was just what I needed. I knew how I felt about Kevin, but I also knew that the commitment would mean compromise in a manner that would test what I believed about living with others and caring enough about them to love them for who they were, as individuals with differing views.

Kevin In a way, I was rather selfish now that I think about it; I wanted to be married to her, but I did not think about the position I was putting her in. She was just married, and her husband was being sent to war where anything could have happened. As it turned out, I made it home safely, but what would have happened to her if I had gotten seriously injured or killed? Everything turned out OK, but she could have had a vegetable for a husband, or I could have been killed and left her a widow. I am glad I made it home safely, though. I have the best wife and friend I could possibly have, and I wonder what I have done sometimes to deserve her. I know that living with me cannot be that easy. Sometimes I get like everyone else, I guess—you know, not at 100 percent, if you understand.

Monica Kevin and I were different as night and day, but the stubbornness, independence, and rebelliousness were characteristics we shared. Acceptance of those characteristics in ourselves was a strong bond, along with something else—I think I'm still trying to figure that something else out. We seemed to understand each other in spite of the fact that we could clearly draw the Mason-Dixon Line through any room we were in. Kevin was from Tennessee, I was from New York. Kevin grew up with country roots and a strong dedication to the values of the South. I grew up on the beaches and in the mountains of New York, never far from the museums, stage productions, and the faster pace of New York City. Kevin makes his point in three short sentences. I can relate experiences for a week. Kevin was very much a red state resident when we met, and I was very much more blue state. In my nightly conversations with myself, I could never understand how two people so different could ever work, and yet I couldn't help feeling myself more drawn to the possibility of it working, even as my head told me it didn't make sense.

I finally came to understand that we were being given a chance to have the kind of relationship I had often hoped for. In my conversations with the people I cared about, I had laughingly told them all my idea for a perfect relationship. I saw it as two circles, one red and one blue, whose circumstances found a way to bring them together. The circles were different, unique, just as two individuals are. In time, familiarity caused the circles to overlap, as the individuals learned more about the commonality of the values they shared. A part of each of the circles gave a little to the relationship, and the center became colored with purple where their mutual interests joined. If the individuals remembered the strength of their individuality, the red and blue would never be gone completely, but the common center would become a deeper and richer purple because of the strength of the uniqueness that came from each part. A passionate thought for a relationship steeped in reality, and yet it is what I realized Kevin and I had when I looked back at how far we had come. We shared a common dream, but our individual strengths working together were what would get us through the challenges we would face alone in order to achieve the reality of the dream. It would be a journey well worth the difficult times. It was a journey leading to peace.

December 2002

Monica There were several attempts to find more days that we could spend together during the course of the fall before we were married. Between Kevin's army schedules, my schedule at work, and my kids, we never did manage to have any more time together. We continued to talk nightly and write e-mails just as often.

Kevin kept bringing Iraq into the conversation. At this point it was certain that the 4th Infantry would be deployed to Iraq. The 3rd Infantry had already been sent—many units directly from Afghanistan and others from the states. Equipment for Kevin's unit had been loaded on ships and was already heading for the Persian Gulf. Now it was simply a matter of acquiring permission from Turkey for the 4th Infantry to use that country's military bases as a starting point for movement into Iraq in support of the efforts of the 3rd Infantry Division. Almost nightly, Kevin would tell me that he didn't expect to be in the States for Christmas.

Kevin The powers that be could not get anything worked out, it seemed. We were told about every two months starting in August

2002 to be prepared to be gone to Iraq by a certain date. Well, all of those dates came and went, and yet we were not deployed. The ups and downs of being told we would be gone by a certain date were starting to wear down the tolerance levels of the soldiers in my unit. Look at it this way: We heard a date, got ourselves mentally ready to go, prepared our family members, and then we would be told to stand down. We wondered, "When in the hell are we going to be told anything reliable?"

Monica This was a difficult time. There was the responsibility to my children, the commitment I had made to my work, and there were the feelings of concern over what Kevin was facing. Many nights I wondered whether everything I had worked for could be fitted into a life with someone who had been trained to kill people. I took care of the elderly. I helped their families find peace with the fact that the lives of their parents were ending. I helped my residents learn to come to terms with the lives they had lived, reconciling their regrets with their successes and finding peace in their last days. I cared for people who had been fortunate enough to live long lives—who had survived so much pain, hurt, and change, and who spent hours talking about all the history they had witnessed. I watched the ends of lives that had been lived as they were meant to be—giving to families, giving to communities and, in the circumstances of so many veterans that I cared for, giving to their country. These were lives to be honored and valued, for they were the lives of people who had survived. Theirs were lives well lived.

January 2003

Monica Kevin and I were not able to spend time together during the holidays. We continued to talk, and the anticipation of impending deployment and relationship changes made things tense at times. I had decided that what will be, will be, simply because it was what worked. There were aspects of the situation that were out of my control, so I did what I could and kept going. Kevin had said he was moving to Georgia when he returned from Iraq, and if I wanted to go with him, I would have to be ready. I felt that was the direction I was going, but part of me still didn't want to believe that I was really involved with someone who was about to be deployed to war. I spoke with the elderly residents in my care daily; so many were veterans or spouses of veterans. They talked to me about their experiences during war and showed me pictures from their lives during World War II, along with medals and other memorabilia. It was enlightening for me, and it seemed to bring a bit of life back to their eyes at the same time. They were proud of what they had faced back then and how they had faced it. They were not ashamed of their actions—they often became frustrated, even angry to a degree, not over having gone to war but over the fact that they had not been able to stop war.

Kevin The men and women Monica speaks of who served during World War II gave her much advice and looked out for her when I could not. I am very grateful to these people, and I don't even know how to tell them just how much. I hope they sense in their hearts just how much they did for us and what it means to me, because I don't have the right words to tell them.

Monica One of the residents I cared for had been a prisoner of war during World War II. I took care of this man for two years, and in that time his wife had become family to me as well. In the months before his dementia became debilitating, we would sit together. He would talk about his experiences, but only to a point. There was always an edge he wouldn't walk past, and I knew it was painful for him. He had been a bomber pilot with a crew of eighteen. They had been shot down, and yet every man had returned home after a period of time in captivity. Every year the group would meet to remember, and it didn't stop when this man moved to the facility where I worked. They were proud, dignified, and respectful of not only their service but the service of the military today. They respected what Kevin was doing. They understood his reasons, and they appreciated that he wanted to serve. They did not want war, and they hoped that it would not come. I don't think people really gave much thought to what this war caused our veterans to face. So many had already been through the worst that war could bring, and with all of the media coverage leading up to the invasion, they would all go through those memories again in a very vivid manner.

Kevin The men at the facility where Monica worked had been to war, and they had seen the stupid brutality of it. They knew that we should not be having any more, and they were at a loss as to why we still fight wars. I am with them 100 percent after my firsthand experience with war and all its baggage. If we are the advanced and enlightened people we claim to be, then why are we still engaging in war?

Monica While caring for this man and learning what it meant to him to serve his country, I also watched what it meant to be the wife of someone who had made that commitment. This woman was a very strong lady and someone I learned to respect very much. She had stood by her husband even while he was lost to her for two years as a prisoner of war—the result of a deployment that happened only a few short weeks after they were married. At the end of his life, she stood by him again. Watching them together, I realized that commitment was hard to find anymore, and I wanted to be that strong.

On January 16 Kevin called me and said that his unit was scheduled to deploy that weekend. If I wanted to see him again before he left, I would have to find a way to get to Fort Hood before the weekend. That was a crossroads for me. There was not any more time to let things take their course. I left instructions for my care staff, packed a bag, and drove to Fort Hood two days later with no idea of what to expect.

It was difficult to find a hotel room in Killeen, the closest town to Fort Hood, but I did finally succeed. There was clearly a sense of impending deployment. Soldiers were busy packing up barracks rooms, signs posted on local businesses offered quick prayers for the safety of the troops, and people gave soldiers in uniform quick glances of respect when they passed. I sat on the built-in bunk in the barracks room and watched Kevin packing the few boxes of his gear. I had never spent time in a soldier's barracks before. I had never seen soldiers prepare for war before, never even given it a thought—not from the perspective I now had. It was surreal in a way. I was part of all of it, but still on the outside of it—like watching a movie. It didn't seem real, because I hadn't allowed myself to feel the reality of what I was facing. There I was, the safety of my world about to be shattered in ways I could never dream, and while my head thought I wanted to stop it, there was something else that said I could not.

Kevin finished packing. We returned to the hotel for the night. It was quiet. What do you say when war is looming?

The next morning we drove on post and Kevin reported to an accountability formation. During the last days before deployment many formations like this one are called throughout the day. At this formation Kevin's unit was told that plans had changed. The impending deployment had been postponed, and there was no word on when it would be rescheduled. The soldiers were to continue as they were until their command received further orders.

This brought a sense of relief. There were questions to be asked, decisions to be made, and plenty of thinking to be done. This changed everything. War changes everything.

I stayed in Killeen for the remainder of the weekend, then returned home to work the following week. My residents were relieved, and yet many seemed to know that it was all just beginning. My going to Killeen seemed to break through a barrier. It meant I was now emotionally involved in what I had sought to keep outside my range of feeling.

The next two months brought change. There were considerations that I never thought would cross my mind, choices to work through, and plans to be made. Most days, except for work and the kids, it seemed as if everything were being done for me, totally out of my control, and I let that continue. It was what worked; with so many new thoughts coming at me so quickly, there was nothing else that would.

No one knew when the 4th Infantry would now deploy. There was even talk that the division would not deploy and that another would go in its place. Back then, I was still on the outside of all this, to a degree. With the chance to back out at any time, for me nothing would be lost. I know now what soldiers and their families feel—the waiting with no knowledge of what is coming can be almost unbearable.

February 2003

Monica I went back to Fort Hood every weekend, leaving for work on Monday morning when Kevin left for the unit's first formation. What had been a long-distance relationship—one that could still be molded to be what it needed to be—quickly became a close relationship, and the thoughts became more confusing. Not only were we working on a relationship, but we were also dealing with our feelings about war, real war, and the fact that it was now inevitable. Every Monday that I left meant we were one weekend closer to hearing that deployment was rescheduled, and the soldiers were being told they would be gone for a year.

On February 3 I packed to make the trip to Fort Hood again. Kevin had told me what some of his favorite meals were, and I brought a different one with me back to Killeen each week for a break from mess hall dining. We spent the weekend after formations driving around the area outside Fort Hood—and talking. A recreation area for the soldiers and families had a beautiful man-made lake with nature trails, camping, outdoor activities, deer, and ducks. It wasn't used as much in the colder weather, so it was a quiet place to deal with emotions and try to make sense of a very unsettling situation.

Kevin Getting those home-cooked meals from Monica was the highlight of my week many times, and I appreciated them immensely. And being able to spend time with her at the lake and the other places we were able to get away to and have some quality time together were moments that I will never forget.

Monica It was getting more frustrating for the soldiers. Kevin was at the point where he just wanted to leave for Iraq to get the deployment over with, and it seemed to be the state of mind for most of the other soldiers as well. People say that everyone has challenges in life, and since soldiers volunteered, they should face theirs quietly. There are challenges, and no one can say what constitutes a difficult challenge for each person. I have been through many, but war changes everything.

Some people say that soldiers should simply face what they're doing and stop doing it, while others say they should feel proud of the sacrifices they are making. I've been in the civilian world—I lived and breathed the civilian world, completely separated from anything having to do with the military. I knew soldiers existed, but what they did rarely crept into my mind. I knew soldiers from past wars—the veterans of the world wars and the Korean War and a few from Vietnam. I knew of the honor, the sense of duty, and the responsibility they talked about feeling for their service to defend their country and its freedoms. It would have been just as easy for *me* to look at a soldier and say, "Stop now," at one point in my life, before I was aware of what their service really meant to them.

Kevin The people who have never worn the uniform have no right to criticize the people who have, in any way. You cannot understand what it is to be a soldier and to serve your country in this manner unless you have done so. The ones who say the troops should take whatever they get and say nothing about it are way off the mark with that type of attitude. I would say that nine times out of ten, they are the ones who cry the loudest over the most insignificant things that happen to them in the civilian world. If these people had to face the things that soldiers do, they would be on the floor, whimpering.

Monica Walking around Fort Hood, listening to Kevin and watching him with the other soldiers, watching soldiers and their families prepare for such a difficult time ahead, not yet fully realizing just how difficult it would be, I was waking up to a new perspective. I was learning—and what I learned was a respect for people who had made such a serious commitment to what they believed, not only in the past but in the present—my present. I was proud of what these men believed in, and even though I was unsure of the reason for this war, I knew that the soldiers I met were committed to what they had chosen to do. They believed in themselves, their values, and what they served to defend. I knew that those outside the military—both those who urged the soldiers forward and those who protested against what they were about to do—had no idea who these men were or why they served, unless they had also served or walked closely by them, immersed in the lives they led.

On February 10 Kevin left at 5 a.m. for early morning formation, and I slept a little longer. When he came back from formation, it was clear there was still no word on deploying. Kevin said he'd had enough. He was not waiting any longer, and that day we were married. I was quite at peace with it—it was the next step.

Kevin I was not waiting any longer; I knew I wanted to marry Monica. Originally I wanted to wait until I returned from Iraq, but I did not see us going anytime soon. I felt that the powers that be could not pull their heads out of their fourth point of contact long enough to do anything with any organization or coherence.

Monica The next day, I left for home and work. For the next month, this became a way of life. Thursday I would pack the truck and drive to Fort Hood. Monday morning I would leave to return south in time for an afternoon of work.

2: Deployment

Monica We took this time as a gift. We used every minute we had to make memories and talk about plans for when Kevin redeployed. It must have been difficult for Kevin, because he was caught between making sure to have time for me and fulfilling his responsibilities as a soldier. I wasn't sure what he was thinking about Iraq. I didn't ask. I just waited for him to talk, and I sensed that there were things he didn't say. I know he was trying to keep me from being hurt, just as much as I was trying to give him good things to remember when he was in Iraq. Neither one of us really knew what Iraq would be like. Who could know? None of us knew.

We fit as much into this time as we could. One weekend we spent camping. One weekend was spent fishing. We lived in a great little furnished efficiency for five days and spent time in a cabin in the woods that sat away from everyone and everything. We had a pasture full of cows to walk in, deer tracks to follow, marshmallows to toast, and stars to watch. The water in the lake was cold, but bundled up in the warmest clothes and trolling just offshore in a little fishing boat brought memories I wouldn't trade.

Five weekends went by, and it seemed as if we created a lifetime in a very short time. March 23 came, and the memories were going to have to last. Kevin's unit had finally received its deployment orders. We kept hoping that our leaders would come to their senses. They did not. The atmosphere changed at Fort Hood. Life became serious, and the soldiers became detached as they began their final preparations. Detachment is necessary in order to survive. War changes everything.

On March 28 I drove the truck to Fort Hood with a mixed sense of apprehension and hope. Part of me did not want to believe that the soldiers were really deploying, but the reality had been splashed all over the television screens for the past week and a half. Daily news reports of bombings and air raids in the eerie haze of the night-vision scopes made the apprehension worse. Strength comes to you when you need it. Somehow we would get through this—thousands of us would experience the heartache together, but a world full of millions didn't have a clue.

Kevin and I spent the night camping, talking, and looking at the stars. We spent the next two days and nights in transition. In between formations and meetings, we spent time packing last-minute belongings from the barracks to be taken to a storage room. We ate pizza and talked. Soldiers from his unit stopped by and shared their feelings over what they were about to do. None of the soldiers seemed sure of the war; they were only sure that they had made a commitment and they would see it through.

On March 30 Kevin received his final orders: He would deploy that night and was to report to final formation at the arms room to draw weapons at 1 a.m. We slept for a while and then, in the shadow of one small light, I watched while he put on his uniform and made a final check of his knapsack and duffel bag. With classic rock playing in the background, it was a strange feeling to watch the chemical suit, chemical antidotes, and gas mask being stowed away, while knives were placed in boots and hidden pockets. I tore pieces of paper, wrote notes, and stuffed them in the corners of his bags, inside his camouflage, and at the bottom of his canteen covers so that he could find them when he least expected them. Then time stopped. I thought it strange that it was the middle of the night. I grabbed a pillow and dozed on the front seat of the truck while he drew his weapon and talked with the other soldiers. A few family members of other soldiers were nearby, not as many as I had expected. One of the soldiers had said that he did not want his family there. He did not want to put them through the pain they would feel watching him go to war. I wondered which would be better. I was glad I chose to stay.

Kevin Those little notes Monica put into my pockets and other gear were a very bright spot in the monotony of the slow times in Iraq. I would be looking for something, and I would find one and it was great to have her thoughts with me. I am also glad she chose to stay with me as I was deploying. I think it is hard for people to see their loved ones go to war, but I think it is worse when they are not there to give them one last hug before they leave.

Monica We drove to the convenience store for coffee and hot chocolate, then sat outside the arms room in the truck and drank it quietly just to keep warm. There weren't many words—the silence seemed to say more than words could at that point. We stood under a street lamp and had a final picture taken in the dark. At that point, that was how I felt—in the dark, and somehow, with the dark wrapped around us, it felt as if everything would be OK.

Then came the call for final formation: detachment. The lines were drawn—family now became the outsiders, and all we could do was watch. In the quiet, the units formed. After roll call, the orders were given to march to the gym for the final manifest. In the night, the quiet cadence of hundreds of boots marching in unison seemed to send echoes over the installation. I stood outside the door with the other family members who were there to support their soldiers. It was difficult to tell the soldiers apart in the darkness.

As they walked through the doorway, soldiers were handed a plug to put behind the pin of their M16 to keep it from firing while they traveled. That one small action had more of an impact than I thought—as I watched Kevin go through the door with his equipment and his helmet on, take the plug, and place it in his weapon, I realized what we faced, what we all faced. War.

Moving into the gym, the world changed. Everything was bright, and patriotic music was blaring over loudspeakers. The soldiers formed in the middle of the gym and stood at attention until released. Family members milled around, soldiers were on the phones for last-minute good-byes, and there were signs of every emotion imaginable. I had reached the point of simply wanting it all to start so that it would all be over. Five minutes more and the soldiers were given the order to re-form while family members were ushered out of the building. In a matter of minutes the lines of soldiers began leaving the gym to board waiting buses, engines running to keep warm in the night. It was 3 a.m. and there was no time left.

I found Kevin in line, and then he was out the door. The line between military and civilian was now clearly defined, and I realized that I was totally immersed in a brand new world that I knew very little about. It became very lonely. There was a lot I was about to learn. I never had the feeling that he would be hurt, or worse. I always felt peace for him personally, but I felt apprehension as well. It would be easy to explain those feelings now. The chaos of every aspect of war— from preparations, training, lack of information (all the changes), anticipation—no one can ever know without the experience, just how much of a roller-coaster ride it can be. If the opinions of thousands of people who are not immersed in the reality of the action are added to your own thoughts and feelings, it becomes even more difficult to find a balance. It is important to stay focused on your own experiences and feelings, and not allow others to sway you. To survive in war, on the front lines far from home, or waiting for someone who is, it is important to trust yourself, your conscience, and your beliefs above anything else.

I pulled the truck to a free parking space right next to the bus Kevin was on. I could not see him, but I wanted him to see me and know that I waited as long as I could. As the buses slowly pulled away I followed them for as long as I could before the barricade went up, and I was turned away. I drove for a long time, heading south to work. It was dark and all I could think about was what it must be like to be a soldier, something I had never thought of with so much depth before.

Kevin I saw her waiting by the bus and she looked so lost out there, I wanted to get off the bus and let her know that I was going to be fine one more time, but I could not do that because the bus pulled away. The men on the bus were quiet as we went to the airfield, each with their own thoughts as we were going to war. There was quite a contrast between all the hoopla the army put on at the gym and the atmosphere on the bus. But that is how the army really operates anyway; put on the gleaming image while keeping the reality at bay with shiny bells and whistles.

Monica War changes everything.

April 2003

Monica During the week after the deployment I received a call at work from a flight attendant who had worked on the flight that Kevin took to Kuwait. She said that she had a message from Kevin that he wanted her to share with me. At least I knew he was in Kuwait.

Kevin The flight attendant promised me she would call Monica and let her know that I had made it safely to Kuwait. I am glad she kept her word. I don't know her name, but I owe her a very big thanks. The flight crews of all the flights it took to get us there were going out of their way to do all they could for us because they knew that some of us would not be coming back.

Monica This was the beginning of the war. There was no Internet access for soldiers, the mail system was not yet in place, and we had no idea when we would have any sort of communication. Kevin did manage to make a call on the night before his unit left Kuwait and moved into Iraq. I missed that call. At work the next day I received a call from the father of a soldier who served as the driver of Kevin's M113 (armored personnel carrier). He wanted me to know that Kevin had asked him to reach me to let me know that he did not know when he would be in contact again. This man was retired military. He made sense of what was happening. I wished I had been able to talk to Kevin.

Kevin Being in Kuwait was strange because it really brought home what we were about to do. It was also nerve-wracking in a way, as I did not know what to really expect from war. We were in Kuwait for about two weeks to get all our equipment ready to cross the man-made berm of sand separating Kuwait from Iraq. I met a few of the British soldiers there while we were waiting to cross. They were anxious to get started back because they had been in Basra, Iraq, and they felt as if they had some more to do.

While we were getting all the stuff needed to go to war, Scud missile attack alerts from a loud siren announced the incoming missile. We had about seven or eight of these alerts while we there; fortunately, our Patriot missile batteries were able to blow those things out of the sky before they could land on us.

I remember it was kind of humorous that after the alerts (which required our donning gas masks and chemical suits because we did not know at the time if there were chemical or biological weapons in the missiles), we would receive the all-clear announcement over the PA system of the compound. This announcement would come after the chem/bio teams did a thorough check of the area to ensure there was nothing present. The humorous part was that the British contingent would announce the same thing about ten minutes later. I told my buddies that the British were waiting to see if any of the "bloody stupid Yanks" would start flopping around before they took off their protective gear.

We saw some rather amazing sights and heard a lot of stuff while we were there. After we had crossed the berm and were making our way toward Baghdad, we came across some small missiles that were on trailers in a lot to the west of the city. One of the scouts in a Bradley Fighting Vehicle requested permission to "engage the target" (which I still haven't figured out since there was no one manning these missiles). At any rate, they pumped a few high-explosive antitank rounds into these missiles, and one of them lifted off the trailer it was on and left in a hurry, trailing yellow smoke behind it. I thought we had found the hidden weapons of mass destruction (WMDs) and unleashed them on ourselves. I immediately put on my mask and watched the other guys who were just watching in awe as it went up. I still do not know where that missile landed.

Monica While Kevin was deployed I learned a lot about the military. The residents I cared for remembered so much of their time at war.

The women talked about what they had done to stay busy, and the men spoke of what Kevin and the other soldiers would be going through. They talked more of what war felt like and how they had dealt with it. They offered a perspective that Kevin would not have been able to at the time. Detachment was necessary for survival in the middle of a combat zone. We watched the news broadcasts of the events in Iraq, and the veterans offered their wisdom in response to every question asked.

The women I cared for brought out scrapbooks filled with memories, proud to talk about the service they and their husbands had given. They encouraged me to stay busy; of course, work and kids did that, but they had other ideas as well. I was soon making a quilt to have ready when Kevin came home, and crocheting as well. It wasn't long before a number of the residents were crocheting again, as well as painting, cooking, and sewing.

The time went quicker than I thought it would, and my many "grandparents" taught me well. I came to respect their wisdom and have many treasured creations to keep me from forgetting that year.

May 2003

Monica Almost three months passed before I heard from Kevin after the deployment from Fort Hood. He was finally given access to a satellite telephone. The call lasted about five minutes and there was a delay before every exchange of conversation, but at least I knew he was safe.

I mailed letters every day and care packages every week, and had done so since the day he deployed. It took almost three months for him to receive the first of what I had sent. For the entire time he was deployed at least a month passed between the time a communication was sent and received. Phone calls were sporadic, at best, and I found myself leaving my cell phone on all the time. People became accustomed to my leaving meetings to take calls, just in case it was Kevin. I wore his BDU (Battle Dress Uniform) jacket as a smock at work, and a yellow ribbon in my hair every day. I wanted people to know that Kevin was serving, and the residents I cared for made sure to mention him to visitors as well. I learned from them. War is difficult, but at the time, it was for a cause the soldiers believed in. While the veterans were uncomfortable with our having gone to war, they understood the commitment and the need to be there for the soldiers who now served.

Kevin Receiving those packages was a blessing to me and some of my buddies because it was a little taste of home. Monica would pack some homemade cookies and other things that were readily available at home but hard to come by in Iraq. We had adopted a wild dog while we were in Khanaqin and we named him Ralph, after a dog from the Looney Tunes cartoons. Monica even sent some dog biscuits for him because I had told her about him,

• • •

Commendation Medals

Monica During the time that Kevin was deployed, he received two Army Commendation Medals for his service. In making their recommendations for Kevin's first Commendation Medal, awarded for the months from March to May 2003, those in his chain of command gave these comments, in part:

> Sgt. Benderman distinguished himself while preparing the Troop's M3A3 Bradley fleet for combat operations. His efforts played a vital role in C Troop being the first Troop in the Squadron ready to LD (cross the line of departure) and the first company-sized element from the 4th ID [Infantry Division] to enter Iraq.
>
> Sgt. Benderman elevated his level of performance in order to secure mission success for the Troop. Trained to work on Bradley Fighting Vehicles, he became a competent maintainer of every type vehicle in the Troop. As a result of his initiative and technical competence, crews often asked for Sgt. Benderman by name to perform maintenance on their vehicles.

In awarding the second Commendation Medal representing his two years of active duty with the 4th Infantry Division, the chain of command stated, in part:

While deployed in Operation Iraqi Freedom, Sgt. Benderman's attention to detail and situational awareness ensured that his soldiers and their equipment were accounted for at all times. His risk reductions factors ensured that there were no injuries or damage to equipment during all operations.

Sgt. Benderman has mentored one soldier to attend the soldier of the month board, two soldiers toward promotion, and one in receiving his spurs last April. He continues to keep his soldiers geared toward career advancement and education. He has built a team and trained his soldiers to look beyond their current rank and achieve at that next level.

Monica Kevin was a dedicated soldier. Every soldier I met who served with Kevin respected his service and trusted his leadership. When Kevin left Iraq, the soldiers in his company presented him with a replica of the guidon that represented the 1-10 Cavalry unit Kevin was attached to during his combat tour. I could tell this meant a lot to him. It was from the soldiers he worked with, and I knew that their respect was something that mattered to him.

• • •

Monica During this time period, Kevin became increasingly concerned with orders his unit received that were out of their realm of training and preparedness. On several occasions, the unit's mechanics were called upon to use their maintenance vehicles and retrieve unexploded ordnance to be destroyed by "sappers" (explosives experts) of their unit. This became more of a concern as Kevin watched members of his unit being seriously injured on several of these missions. At this point, Kevin wrote letters to his congressmen in Tennessee, reporting his concerns for the safety of his soldiers, which he forwarded to me so that I could send them to the appropriate congressional offices. Not knowing why at the time, I made copies of the letters before I mailed them. We did eventually learn that one of them, at least, had been read and forwarded to the Department of the Army for further investigation.

Kevin The incident that really sticks out in my mind as one of the dumbest things that happened while we were there was when our first sergeant ordered two soldiers (a specialist 4th class and a private 1st class from the mortar platoon) to gather a large cache of enemy mortar rounds and load them onto a five-ton truck. We had located these weapons at a site we code-named Tinderbox because it was a large ammo dump. Anyway, while the soldiers were carefully loading these mortar rounds onto the truck (for those of you who don't know, a mortar round is an impact weapon that detonates after it lands nose first on the target), the first sergeant came to check on the progress. I suppose he thought the soldiers were moving too slow, so he told the soldiers to hurry up and throw the rounds onto the truck. Any of you reading this that has been in the army can guess what happened next. The young soldiers, being junior soldiers, immediately obeyed the order from the first sergeant and started tossing the rounds into the truck. Well, one of the fuses exploded on one of the mortars and sent shrapnel flying into the two young soldiers. Fortunately they were not killed, as it was only the fuse that exploded. This is when I decided to write my congressmen to let them know these kinds of things were happening during the course of my deployment.

Another thing that made me realize that some of the people I went to war with looked at it like it was a big game was the fact that the maintenance team had been told to recover missiles using the M88 Recovery Vehicle to do so (the missiles were French-made, so maybe that is why France was hesitant about going to war with Iraq). This vehicle is designed, and the people on it are trained, to recover battle-damaged vehicles, and neither it nor its crew members are designed or trained to deal with explosive ordnance. The battalion commander wanted to have these missiles blown up and he ordered the maintenance platoon to load these things onto trucks to be moved to a pit where the sappers would place C-4 plastic (a plastic explosive used by the military) around them and blow them up in the pit. I've seen photos of some of the maintenance soldiers sitting on top of the missiles and pretending to ride them like they were cowboys on a bronco or something, but I do not have access to these photos to present them here.

Monica After two months in country, Kevin's unit finally settled into position in a small town near the Iranian border, Khanaqin. The company planned on setting up its base in an old abandoned customs building. It was surrounded by a cement wall, and most of the building was in a shambles because whoever left it did so in a hurry. As the soldiers began setting up camp, children from the village of Khanaqin would climb on the wall surrounding the building to watch what they were doing. The soldiers had not yet placed the concertina wire on top of the wall, so they kept waving the children off the wall, telling them to get away.

This went on for a while, until finally the commander of Kevin's unit came out of the customs building and told the soldiers, "If those kids get back up on the wall again, I want you to shoot them."

Kevin said that he was appalled, as were all the members of his unit who heard the commander. No one acted on the order. Kevin felt that fear and concern for the situation they were in caused the man to say what he did, but Kevin's worry was that this captain was even able to make this statement.

Kevin This was one of the most amazing statements I heard while I was there. To have my company commander come out of the building and actually order us to shoot children who were doing nothing more than being children was beyond belief. The guys who heard it and I were in no way going to shoot small children who were doing nothing more than tossing small pebbles and laughing. We all just looked at him like he was out of his mind, and he turned around and went back inside the building. I cannot figure out why he said this unless he was just scared and not thinking about what he was saying.

After a while our company commander was due to be replaced, as his time for being a company commander was nearly up (you only get a year as a company commander), and his replacement arrived. This captain continued having our soldiers doing things that were in no way mission essential. An incident comes to mind: They had found a statue of Saddam Hussein on a horse, and the captain decided he wanted it, so he had it brought back to our maintenance compound.

The horse was anatomically correct, and the captain wanted to "neuter" the horse so he could present the result as an award to the tank or Bradley crew who performed best during firing exercises.

Here we were in the middle of the war and this idiot wanted to play college kid games.

I met many interesting people while I was there; I met a man named Mr. Sadullah (I hope I spelled his name correctly) who was providing for his sister and her six children and a mentally handicapped brother. Mr. Sadullah is a teacher at the school in Khanaqin and earns $40 a month. He was providing for himself and all of those people on that salary. This man befriended us while we there and would invite us to his home for meals, which amazed me because he wanted to have the entire company of soldiers (about two hundred; as it was, he would take about ten to twelve on a regular basis) to eat with him at his expense. This man was living in a war zone and taking care of his family and he wanted to treat us like honored guests. I felt as if I should be buying things to give to him, but in Iraq it is considered bad manners to offer gifts or money when someone invites you to a meal.

I met a man who spoke six languages and held an engineering degree from Baghdad University. I met construction workers, auto mechanics, plumbers, electricians, farmers, and a wide variety of people who are very much like people I know here at home. The image that I held of these people as backward heathens living in the past was dispelled after I got to know some of them. Yes, they do hold on to some of the traditional ways of doing things, but what is wrong with that? I think we should have kept some of the traditions we had here in America; I feel we would be better off if we had.

August 27, 2003

Monica Kevin returned from Iraq with little notice. He was told about a week prior that he was to be sent home. He had called near the end of July to tell me that it appeared he might be redeployed early. He had reenlisted prior to the invasion and was scheduled to be reassigned to the 3rd Infantry at Fort Stewart, but his stop-loss orders kept him at Fort Hood to deploy with his unit there. The 3rd Infantry had received its redeployment orders to finally return home, after over a year of service first in Afghanistan and then Iraq, and its soldiers were more than ready to return. I had been communicating with some of the spouses of 3rd Infantry soldiers over the summer. Just as we had felt the apprehension over waiting to hear word of when the 4th Infantry would be heading to Iraq, the 3rd Infantry soldiers and families faced even greater apprehension as plans to return home were continually changed on short notice. It has now become evident that Kevin was sent home early because he was causing so many problems for his commanders in Iraq. He asked questions, wrote to congressmen about his concerns, and did not blindly follow orders he knew to be wrong.

Kevin The return flights went fast and slow, if you understand what I mean. There were a couple of stops on the way for refueling. The first one was near the Mediterranean and the second one was in Shannon, Ireland, where they let us off the plane and we were able to get a cold beer. Those beers were good and went down smoothly. But I was anxious to get home to Monica.

Monica I had expected Kevin to be home a week later than he arrived. Once again a phone call interrupted another meeting I was in. It was a sergeant from Fort Hood calling to tell me that the flight Kevin was on was currently en route from Ireland. He would be on the ground at two that next morning. I remember wondering if the army ever did anything during daytime hours. Not thirty minutes after hanging up from that conversation, I had another. It was Kevin calling to surprise me. He was already in Boston waiting for the next connection home. I told him I had heard from the sergeant at Fort Hood—and then part of me wished I hadn't said a word. I finished my work, quickly went home to pack a few essentials, and drove the five hours to Fort Hood. A new kind of apprehension set in. We had talked as much as we were able during the deployment, but I knew there was much I didn't know. I wondered how war zones changed a person and I wondered if I would be able to understand what had happened. We were already having questions about what this war was about. I could tell in some of Kevin's letters that he was asking himself questions as well. He had talked a bit about his father's service in World War II. I had heard a few stories of his father's own beliefs about war. I was certain Kevin would have been reminded of these conversations during his time in Iraq. Once again, change was coming. War has a way of doing that.

When I got to Fort Hood it was almost 2 a.m. The installation is one of the largest in the army—I was lost. After getting directions from some enthusiastic military police, I found my way to the parking lot and pulled up next to the line of buses that had already arrived, bringing soldiers back. There was equipment all over the parking lot. I went inside to look for Kevin but couldn't find him. My first thought was that he had not arrived. Once again veterans were there with the wisdom of their experience. This time they were helping with the homecoming and they knew just where to look to find Kevin. It didn't take long for the apprehension to dissipate.

I can understand, now, what it means to be part of the military. I am proud of having been there and proud of Kevin's service. War does change everything, but not everything is changed for the worse.

September 2003—Fort Stewart, Georgia

Monica Kevin had to remain at Fort Hood until he had completed what was called "out processing." The paperwork required by the military is amazing. Once again we found ourselves in transition. We stayed in a cabin on the recreational facility near post, traveling south on weekends to pack and spend time with family. It wasn't long before the work in Texas was done. Nothing is ever easy, unless you live your life committed to nothing. But that's not really living. We were about to embark on another difficult journey, but having gotten through Iraq, it seemed that we could make it through this as well.

January 2004

Monica After two months of getting acquainted with our new community and a new military installation (Fort Stewart), we finally began to settle into life together. It wasn't long before we had a routine, but there was something unsettled as well. Kevin didn't talk much about Iraq. He had written very little of the specifics in the letters he sent home, and the phone conversations were never long enough for much more than reassurances that everything was still all good.

Something I learned from the people I had cared for (or was it they who had cared for me?) is that it's important to have a place that remains the same, what most would call "home." A soldier at war has to have the memory of what was left behind and the assurance that the reality of that memory will not have changed upon returning to it. It's as if time stands still in a way. The days and weeks move forward, but the part of life that was shared comes to a standstill until you are sharing it together again.

While Kevin was in Iraq I felt it was important to keep my same routine so that while he was away, he would know what was happening at home just by thinking about the time, the day, the month. Order. It seems that is how to maintain a sense of peace, even when your duty has thrust you into the most chaotic force imaginable.

To survive a situation as chaotic as war, war cannot be allowed to change everything.

With Kevin deployed I changed as little as possible, and I tried to always be available for his calls. That connection was an important survival tool for both of us.

Now we had moved. Everything had changed. Every aspect of our life seemed new and different, and it took time to establish a new routine. Once in place, however, the existence of the routine seemed to open the door to thoughts that had been pushed aside since Kevin's return. There was now room for questions. I still didn't ask any, but I could tell from Kevin's restlessness that something inside him was questioning. He would have to sort it out. I would listen and watch, but he was going to have to find the answers for himself.

The command of Kevin's new unit at Fort Stewart was pushing him to go to the promotion board. Kevin is a leader and his command recognized his potential. When Kevin rejoined the army after having been away for almost ten years, he returned as a private even though he had left as a specialist when he was honorably discharged in 1991. This meant that even though he had years of active-duty service, two years after returning to the army, he still had to work his way back through the ranks again, making it to the rank of sergeant the year before Iraq. He was more mature than most others in his position, not only because of his age, but also because of his life experiences. His command was working within army regulations to try to move Kevin into the position of leadership they felt he deserved, but also a position that would allow him to have a strong influence over the younger soldiers who served with him. Quite simply, by all recommendations and reports, Kevin was a dedicated, committed soldier who understood his duty and respected the need for discipline in an army where many young soldiers craved his type of leadership.

As stated in the recommendations for the Commendation Medals he had earned during his tour in Iraq, soldiers asked for him by name when their equipment needed maintenance because they trusted him to do the work and ensure their safety. During the time after redeployment when the 3rd Infantry units were rehabilitating the equipment that returned from Iraq with them, Kevin was instrumental in seeing that the work was completed, even with inadequate supplies, records, and accountability.

January 2004

Monica Kevin was recommended by his first line supervisor for the promotion to staff sergeant and was approved to go before the promotion board by the battalion command sergeant major.

Kevin passed the promotion board, which made him eligible for the next rank in the army enlisted hierarchy pending the attainment of the education points necessary to be promoted. The army's promotion system is based on a point system in which a soldier gains points for things like expert marksmanship at the M16 firing range, basic army knowledge, unit history, physical fitness, college credits, leadership skills, and so forth.

February 2004

Monica The 3rd Infantry Division received notice that it would be off-line to redesign the brigades into newly defined Units of Action. Officials at the Pentagon had determined that the army would be more efficient if each battalion was self-contained with support companies, and light and heavy armor companies within each battalion, as opposed to being as specialized as they had been. At this point Kevin's company, Foxtrot Company, 2nd Battalion, 7th Infantry Regiment, was unsure of how it would ultimately realign and what unit it would be attached to.

The new order said Foxtrot would eventually become Delta Company, 3rd Forward Support Battalion.

Kevin met with his first sergeant and was told that he could have the position of training room NCO if he wanted it. This was an administrative position. The NCO assigned to this would be responsible for maintaining training records, soldiers' personnel records, calendars, and schedules for a company of almost two hundred soldiers. At this time the change of duty meant that he would not be moving with his current platoon to 3-69 Armor Battalion but rather that he would stay on as part of a new unit to be formed with the 2-7th Infantry. Kevin had already been considering seeking a noncombat position, so he accepted this offer, as it would take him out of the front lines while he considered the options available to him as far as conscientious objection and receiving an honorable discharge after ten years of dedicated service.

February 2004

Monica From a personal standpoint things were quite comfortable. Our lives moved forward. The kids moved to Georgia to try new lives as well, and we enjoyed taking time to work on gardens and furnish our house. Kevin left for physical training every morning at five and returned afterward for coffee and breakfast before heading back on post to begin work in the motor pool. He was home for lunch and home for dinner every evening. Life happened.

We were peaceful in our relationship, but there was not peace. It wasn't long before we heard the rumbling of a possible return to Iraq. The definitive word never seemed to materialize, but the possibility loomed in everyone's thoughts. The disclaimer was always, "pending conditions on the ground in Iraq."

Kevin requested permission to transfer to the position of training room NCO. It meant more paperwork, but it also meant that he would no longer be near the front lines.

We spent a lot of time walking on the wooded trails that ran throughout the training areas of Fort Stewart. Military personnel have access to over one hundred ponds and thousands of acres of natural areas through the military version of a parks program called Morale,

Welfare, and Recreation. Some of the acreage is reserved for wildlife species that are on the protected registries. Walking with our dogs we had glimpses of snakes, turtles, even a rare eagle, and if it was early enough in the morning, a fox would cross the dirt trail just ahead. There are plenty of deer, wild hogs, and turkeys as well. We would wake in the early mornings to sit along the edge of one of the ponds and fish, watching the sun rise and the natural world waken for the day.

It was a strange juxtaposition of experiences. Sitting at the edge of the pond watching the birds begin to rustle, the early morning stars fading as the sun rose higher in the sky, and the resident alligator slowly sliding its heavy body into the water to cool, we felt peace around us. It was easy to have no thoughts. The quiet was always shattered and thoughts soon crept in as the rumbling of heavy artillery equipment could be heard moving out along a distant trail for training exercises, or the explosion of rounds being fired from Bradleys on the weapons range rumbled as a false thunder.

The "field problems" or training missions that Kevin's company was sent out on for combat preparations became more frequent. Each problem would last for a week, sometimes two. The division was preparing for a two-month training program at the NTC in Fort Irwin, California.

It became easier to see that something was on Kevin's mind now. I would wake up some nights to find him sitting on the couch with the television on quietly, or playing computer games, or even just sitting with one small light on, thinking.

February–April 2004

Monica This was a very confusing time in Kevin's unit. He continued to work in the motor pool with Delta Company because those in charge could not seem to sort out how the reorganization of the division was going to happen. Under this command, Kevin worked as team leader for the motor pool, supervised by a staff sergeant who had little regard for military discipline. This staff sergeant chose to operate a personal computer repair business from the motor pool office. He also had a history of being very bigoted. He had problems with many of the African American soldiers, enough so that many asked to be reassigned. He tried to befriend Kevin. He wanted to take Kevin into his confidence and talked a lot about his feelings about black people and about the military. But he didn't seem to realize that Kevin did not agree with his beliefs and found most of his positions to be offensive. Kevin stood up for the soldiers' best interests, which did not always conform to the decisions of the staff sergeant.

This staff sergeant did not want Kevin to take the training room NCO position. He preferred that Kevin remain as his motor pool sergeant since Kevin did the work and ran the motor pool, allowing the staff sergeant to use his time to run his computer business and leave early for home every day. The staff sergeant was rarely in the motor pool after 2 p.m. Sometimes he didn't return from lunch. It seemed that every time there was an emergency that required a supervisor to return to the motor pool, the staff sergeant was not available, and Kevin had to respond.

During a training problem in the field, this company was out for two weeks at a time. February in Georgia is the rainy season, and it was messy. The staff sergeant would leave the field every night and go home to sleep in his bed, returning to the field in the morning before the command got out there to see that he was missing. Then he would fabricate a story about something he needed in the motor pool and head back to post to sit with his computer business, leaving Kevin and other NCOs to manage the soldiers in the field. The soldiers started talking about this so much that for the next field problem, the staff sergeant worked it out so that he went home every night while the others rotated, leaving Kevin or a second NCO in the field alternately with one group of soldiers so that the other group could spend the night at home.

It appeared that the biggest problem this staff sergeant had with Kevin was that Kevin disciplined the soldiers. The younger, less experienced soldiers in the motor pool would often come to Kevin and ask him how to complete a repair on one of the Bradleys. Kevin's common practice was not to give them a quick answer but to send them to the manuals to learn for themselves. This often frustrated the soldiers because they wanted an easy fix. They would go to the staff sergeant who, in turn, would ride Kevin and tell him that he was too hard on the soldiers. In a sworn statement given to the investigating officer for Kevin's conscientious objector hearing, the staff sergeant verified this, saying he believed that Kevin held the soldiers to a standard that was too high. Kevin's position was that the soldiers would be much better equipped in a combat zone if they would take the time they had available to them during training to learn how to solve maintenance problems on their own. He often asked them, "If I do everything for you, what will you know how to do when I'm gone?"

One young soldier in Kevin's motor pool was arrested off post for shooting at stop signs with a paint gun. The soldier had no vehicle, so Kevin, as his supervisor, was responsible for getting this soldier to court and everywhere else. The soldier was sentenced to eighty hours of community service. Kevin told him to do his community service on weekends and during his time off, and he kept the soldier working in the motor pool. The staff sergeant gave Kevin a hard time about this decision. He wanted Kevin to be easier on this soldier and give the soldier time off to take care of his community service. Kevin thought differently. He thought that the punishment for the crime should be served on the soldier's time off, and that the soldier should continue with his work in the motor pool. It didn't make sense to reward the soldier for breaking a law by giving him time off from work to pay the cost of his error in judgment.

The same staff sergeant who made things so difficult for Kevin in the motor pool was the NCO who ultimately took Kevin to the promotion board, giving him a 100 percent recommendation. He knew Kevin was a strong leader, and he wanted to ensure that Kevin remained in his position as motor pool sergeant by helping to secure Kevin's promotion. When the military intelligence officer, acting as the investigating officer for Kevin's conscientious objector hearing, needed witnesses to testify against Kevin's sincerity, the testimony of this motor pool supervisor contradicted his own documented ratings and recommendations. There were times when the behavior of those in Kevin's chain of command bordered on the ludicrous, and all we could do was shake our heads, hoping that someone, at some point, would see with clarity and change things.

April 2004

Monica From February to April I had five phone conversations, each lasting at least thirty minutes, with the captain who served as the battalion chaplain for the 2-7th Infantry, Kevin's battalion. This chaplain had only been with the battalion for a short time. We talked about my concerns regarding what I saw in Kevin. We also talked about my concerns regarding the Family Readiness Group, the army-created military family support program, and how little the family members of soldiers were supported with any real effort. He and I had several exchanges that he should have remembered, and I am certain that he did, although his later actions would demonstrate how little regard he had for his work and how little commitment he put behind his words. Each time we spoke he offered to help me do something to better the situation for the soldiers' family members. He also said that he would meet with Kevin and discuss what could be done to resolve his personal situation. The chaplain expressed similar concerns about many of the soldiers in the brigade. We talked at length over changes he wanted to see implemented in the support programs, but he claimed that he was unable to begin to make any of these changes, as the battalion was so overworked, and his hands were tied with deployments and unit changes.

Kevin was becoming increasingly frustrated with the lack of leadership in his battalion. It was clear that there was confusion over whose orders were to be followed, and there was little organization in preparation for deploying to the NTC in California. It made little sense that a division that had just returned from yearlong deployments to two different war zones would now, in addition to facing training preparations for the possibility of another deployment in the coming year, be taken off-line to be re-created from the traditional mechanized armored or cavalry units into the new, supposedly streamlined, all-inclusive "Units of Action" that someone in the Pentagon had dreamed up. The confusion this action created simply seemed to interfere with the training the soldiers should have been focused on. All the soldiers seemed to see was dysfunction at the leadership levels, and it did not do much for morale from my perspective.

May 2004

Monica I watched Kevin. I couldn't tell him what to think, nor could I tell him to talk to me if he wasn't ready or didn't want to. I could see that he was thinking. There was a lot that I wanted to say. There were times when I couldn't control the words and he heard clearly what I was thinking, and there were times when I called to express my feelings to family so Kevin did not have to deal with my concerns. I did my best not to push him. Kevin didn't need me adding to his thoughts. I trusted him to know what was best. I had to wait for him to see with the clarity he needed to make the right decision. We watched, listened, and gathered information together. Kevin took it all in and weighed his options with a great deal of deliberation.

Kevin The events I had witnessed in Iraq were a constant reminder to me about the stupidity of war. I was starting to question the factors that are always given as a reason to go to war. I was starting to question the bullshit notion that war makes you a man. Many people who buy that line of garbage will repeat it as if saying it many times will make it true. I have been to war and it doesn't make you a man if you are not one already. It does make you an automaton.

The way we fight wars is sterile compared to the way they were fought in the past. The training we receive is designed to make us look at other human beings as if they were nothing more than cardboard cutouts. I think there would be an entirely different outlook on war if we had to fight the enemy with axes and swords and you had to look people in the eye as you were about to kill them. Now the army uses video games to train soldiers, and it creates the sense that the people we are killing are not real people but images from a game. I think this is wrong because the young people who are taught this in basic and in the training they receive at their permanent posts have to deal with the reality of killing a real person. I think this is what causes so many cases of post-traumatic stress disorder (PTSD) to the degree seen now in the military.

If we are going to continue to fight wars then we should at least train the young men and women who are going to fight them in a realistic manner and take the video-game mentality out of it. Let's tell them the truth—"You will be killing someone who has a family who loves them the way your family loves you"—and let's show the true side of what they are about to do instead of training them to believe it is a game.

Monica We were fortunate to find the house we did to live in. It is not far from town, less rural than many areas on the outskirts of Hinesville, but it is sheltered near the end of a dead-end street so there is little traffic. It is surrounded by Georgia pines and a few tall hardwoods, and it is quiet. We planted gardens out in front, even found room for a small vegetable garden; enough to have a taste of homegrown tomatoes, cucumbers, zucchini, and whatever else we can grow in the small space we pretend is an acre. As cultivated as the front yard is, the backyard remains natural. The trunks of the tall pines are roped with vines of wisteria and muscadine grapes while the ground is covered with pine needles, cones, and wild everything. We built a fountain and added a picnic table. In the evenings we could sit out back with the dogs and not know there was a military installation nearby.

We feed the birds. There's quite a collection of cardinals, chickadees, doves, and jays, along with the migrating species that settle here for a rest before they move farther north or south, depending on the season. It's peaceful in the morning to have a cup of coffee and watch the creatures wake up, and in the quiet it's easier for thoughts to collect and find their place in the midst of the chaos the army seems to naturally bring on.

When it came time for Kevin to leave for NTC, a part of me sensed that it wasn't as easy for him to deploy this time as it might have been in the past. He took longer to get his equipment packed and seemed to have more distractions.

I tried to imagine what it would be like to be a soldier. I will never know. I do know what it's like to be married to one. I don't think Kevin will ever stop being what a soldier is. I think, even as he served in Iraq, he did not serve as a mercenary, as someone trained to kill others. I think Kevin always served as someone who was trained to do whatever it took to defend himself and those he had committed to protect, but who would commit no greater force than necessary to achieve that end. I often think about people with a martial arts background and training in Eastern philosophies. They have the potential and capacity to deal a deadly blow to an enemy, and yet pride themselves on never having to use that physical ability because their mental capacity is always that much stronger. Rather than overcome an enemy with force, they choose to overcome with intelligence. The end result is something that often takes a great deal more time and requires incredible patience, yet it is nonviolent and far more satisfying to achieve a resolution in this peaceful manner.

I always felt that this is how Kevin saw his service in the military. He trained to kill, and to use physical force to destroy an enemy, and yet, in the truest sense of military training, there was also the mental training he instilled in himself—what should have been part of the training that was encouraged the most for all who enlisted to serve. Unfortunately, it was this lack of commitment by army commanders to the mental, psychological, and philosophical strengthening of the human beings who became our nation's defenders that ultimately made Kevin question what the army had asked him to do, and to reevaluate his continued service in light of the principles of morality he chose to hold as his standard for living.

May – July 2004 — National Training Center

Monica The battalion left for Fort Irwin and NTC beginning on May 11. Kevin left on May 17 and the battalion returned on June 29. During the time in NTC, the battalions made the changes that had been talked about since the beginning of the year. Soldiers who left with the 3-69 Armor and the 2-7th Infantry and were scheduled to rotate to their new units did so while at the training center. Kevin went to NTC still working in the motor pool of Delta Company, but as soon as the training missions began, he was assigned to the tactical operations command, and spent all of NTC with the Foxtrot Company executive officer. He had a laptop computer to use while at Fort Irwin and was supposed to be entering the soldiers' readiness information for the new company, but he could not. The information was not yet available. At this point, the company commanders were in heated discussions with each other over who was to command the units, even yelling at each other in front of the enlisted soldiers.

Kevin This was a pathetic joke as we watched the captains fighting like little kids over who was in charge of the company. These were supposedly the men who were going to lead us into battle in a war zone and here they were squabbling like two old ladies. How could they expect the soldiers to have any respect for them if they were going to act like this?

Monica When the units got back to Fort Stewart they had block leave scheduled through July. This was a period of time when each soldier would be given the chance to take time away from post. Kevin took his from July 1 to July 15. When he returned to work, there were still no company offices and no equipment. Kevin had a laptop to do the work on but could not print out any of the documents needed by the company. He had to share a printer with the first sergeant who was never at the company area. He would not let Kevin into his office to use the printer while he was gone, and when he was present, Kevin still could not use it. There was no prior information on any soldiers; it all had to be entered from scratch, and this unit had about one hundred twenty soldiers when it stood up.

There were no dates, no calendars, very little information for Kevin to create the documents needed. The chain of command pushed Kevin to put together training records even though there was nothing to use to accomplish this. This new company was unable to access many of the needed supplies. The supply sergeant had been issued a credit card, but it wasn't activated so it couldn't be used. In November, members of the command actually gave an order to the soldiers in the unit, telling them they would all receive counseling statements if they did not buy their own tape and paint marks to identify the equipment they were sending to Iraq. The army should have supplied this, but the unit had none. Kevin reported this to the command sergeant major, who counseled the first sergeant that this was not something that could be expected of the soldiers.

Kevin I would do as much as possible with what we had at the time. We did not even have a proper office. We were using some rooms that were available in the motor pool and they did not even have any furniture in them. I went around Fort Stewart to other companies and scrounged some old desks, chairs, and filing cabinets that were going to be thrown away because the other companies had requisitioned new furniture. I used my own vehicle to accomplish what I did, and yet the commander had the balls to say that I did not do enough for the new company.

So here we were without the equipment or supplies to set up a new company, and the senior leaders were more concerned with insignificant and petty details while the NCOs and enlisted men were trying to do what they needed without any help from command.

July 2004

Monica Kevin's unit returned from NTC, and he was now listed as being the training room NCO for the 2-7th Infantry, Foxtrot Company, under the command of a new captain who had just been reassigned.

While Kevin was at the NTC he continued to express his frustration with the lack of leadership and the lack of organization. He had the opportunity to call when the cell phone had a signal, and he talked about his concerns over simple training issues. He had tried to talk to the battalion chaplain while at the training center, and did finally manage to have one brief conversation with the man.

I watched a short training documentary created by a psychiatrist who had spent six months in Iraq setting up mental health centers for the military. This man, who had been attached to an Oregon National Guard unit, commented that many of the chaplains in Iraq felt their hands were tied by the commanders of the units, just as the mental health professionals were. They talked with many soldiers who had questions and asked for help, but the commanders did not want their soldiers taken out of active duty for counseling. Many commanders refused to acknowledge soldiers' questions and would not allow their chaplains the latitude to do their work. For many commanders, according to this doctor, it was more important to keep soldiers on the front lines than to attend to their consciences, or their emotional needs.

In retrospect, I believe this was the case with Kevin's battalion chaplain. He was too new to the military, and to Kevin's unit, to have any influence over the command when working with a soldier who questioned actions that affected his conscience. Even had the chaplain been willing to see the truth of what Kevin was saying, the command of Kevin's unit was not going to allow Kevin to make the choices regulations gave him and the Constitution granted as an inalienable right to conscience. In the eyes of this command, Kevin's actions brought public attention to the weaknesses of the command and its personal characters. This was something his command could not allow. The commanders became even more determined to bring Kevin back into their control in an effort to prevent their own fallibilities from becoming an obstacle to their careers.

August 2004 — Preparing for Expiration of Term of Service (ETS)

Monica Kevin had made up his mind at the end of August 2004 to schedule his ETS and initiated the paperwork to get out of the army. We attended two mandatory separation meetings about finances and job searches. It was at this time that Kevin learned he was being ordered to report to BNCOC, the Basic Noncommissioned Officer Course, a secondary leadership training course at Fort Knox, Kentucky, but he requested the order be withdrawn. Being scheduled for ETS, it didn't make sense for him to attend this leadership course. The order was withdrawn. This was something the command did not consider in their assessment that Kevin's actions were merely meant to avoid duty in Iraq. The assignment to BNCOC would have extended through the time his unit would be in Iraq. If Kevin had simply been trying to avoid hazardous duty, all he had to do was attend BNCOC.

September 2004 — Began Search for Conscientious Objector Information

Monica We initially began making phone calls about conscientious objector applications during this time, as Kevin was still being shuttled back and forth from training room NCO to the motor pool. Soldiers have two options for filing for conscientious objector status: They can receive a full discharge, leaving the military and relinquishing rights to all benefits they have accrued during their time of service, or they can continue to serve as a conscientious objector in a supportive role outside combat. Kevin considered at this time filing for 1-A-O (noncombatant) status, thinking that he would deploy but be in a noncombat position until his ETS date.

From August, when the chaplain returned from block leave, through December, Kevin initiated a series of e-mails with him, in which he requested meetings and had exchanges about his beliefs. The chaplain would not meet with Kevin, although I have little doubt that he took all of these exchanges and shared them with the company commander. Kevin tried several times to arrange a meeting with the chaplain so that he could talk with him about the conscientious objector process, but there was always an excuse and nothing was ever done.

September 2004 — Change

Monica Kevin began talking more about his beliefs and his concerns with issues he and the other soldiers faced. As he filed his paperwork to begin the process necessary for his ETS in 2005, he seemed to detach himself a little more from his commitment to the military.

I had to be careful. I did not want Kevin to make his decision based on what he thought I wanted. I had cared for many people in my work and listened to many stories of reconciliation. Men and women who had expressed so many regrets because they had lived their lives for others, making decisions they felt would make others happy but not necessarily themselves, taught me valuable lessons I didn't want to forget. Always putting the desires of others first, many of them felt regret in not taking the opportunity to live for themselves until it was too late to go back and change things. I had found myself doing this for most of my adult life, until I learned that we cannot make another person happy unless we are honest with ourselves and the personal choices we make. Life does not work when we make choices for ourselves that are meant to keep others happy, simply to keep them around and keep ourselves from being alone. Life works best when we make the choices that are right for us, and those who share what we share become part of our life honestly, with no coercion. I was at peace. I had finally come to live by the standards I had set for myself.

I had chosen what I believed to be the truth, and it gave me peace. I wanted this for Kevin. I loved the man, even when the man was a soldier at war. I knew the commitment with which he served, and I knew the principles he stood for. It was very difficult, sometimes, to keep my thoughts to myself and there were times when I couldn't do it. But I did my best to find other outlets. People had cared about me enough to allow me to decide how I wanted to live my life. I chose my life. It would have been very wrong for me not to do the same for those I cared about, even if their choices were not choices I would make. With real love comes trust; you can't have one without the other. If we can't love people enough to trust their ability to make the choices that are best for them, then how can we say we love them at all?

In the ongoing discussion about "supporting the troops," many people we talk to say they could never do so as long as the troops remain in a combat zone; they can only support those who refuse to fight. This, to me, is an essential discussion, one that we all must have beyond its significance regarding soldiers fighting this war. I believe it is a discussion that goes directly to the essence of conscientious objection, and the basis of the laws of humanity, which are the foundation of our Constitution.

When we look at people, I believe we should do our best to look for their inherent good. It's there in all of us, just as the ability to make mistakes is there. Good must be nurtured, however. Good, like strong plants in a garden, must receive care to stay strong. When people are put in difficult situations and the connection with those who have the greatest potential to nurture that good is nearly severed, it is easy for negative thoughts to creep in. Defense mechanisms kick in, and trust in good memories and connections is easily lost when there is nothing to give them hope that the good will not be destroyed in the madness. This happens to all of us, oftentimes in the most mundane circumstances. Fear causes it, along with doubt and the thought of failure, and it happens when we try to control a situation that is not ours to control. Eventually we fail. It is inevitable.

Soldiers are in the worst situation possible when they are immersed in a combat zone like Iraq for months at a time, with no real connection to the aspects of their lives that have the potential to nurture the good and keep them from losing their trust in it altogether.

We can support the soldiers and not support their actions. If we do not, we stand to lose many more soldiers, not just to improvised explosive devices and gunshot wounds. We will lose their trust. We have already lost the trust of many who return hoping those back home have continued to nurture the good they have tried to fight for, only to learn that very few really cared.

When Kevin was in Iraq, I thought about this a lot. I was not for war. I had little real memory of the Vietnam war—only what I had read and seen in movies. I had the conversations with veterans from so many different combat experiences, and I had my conscience. I couldn't kill a spider. I would go to great lengths to catch one in a cup if I found it inside, just to release it in the woods.

We have three geranium pots on our kitchen windowsill. Somehow one fall, a colony of sugar ants found their way through an air space at the bottom of the window and made the geranium pots their new home. They've lived there for a while now. When I accidentally over-water one of the plants, we can soon see a steady stream of tiny ants leaving their flooded home and moving across the windowsill to a drier pot. Eventually they move back. They apparently have their permanent home and one financed by flood insurance. Some people think they don't belong on the windowsill. I believe we coexist, peacefully. The ants are life, just as the spiders, cats, dogs, birds, and any other living, breathing creatures are. We need them, far more than they need us. I often wonder how long it will take for humanity to see that. People talk a good game, but no one really listens, not even to their own words. So—the ants go on, but I wonder how long people will, unless they stop for a moment and learn from the ants.

Every week that Kevin was in Iraq I sent him a care package. I did my best to nurture the good that I knew was harder to find in a war zone. I loved the man, not the war. I loved that he was strong enough to take action to defend what he believed in, even if it meant putting his life in danger. He took action, and I did what I could to help him stay connected to the peace that was waiting back home. I believed in him. There were always requested items to send, but plenty of surprises as well; food treats, silly stuffed creatures to laugh at, books, anything to give him a reminder that home was waiting and it was not changing. I sent a letter every single day, simply to give him a voice from another perspective. I did my best to talk about everything I could think of that had nothing to do with war. He could get the politics and the drama from the news sources I included. I did my best to see that he didn't lose sight of peace.

I think this is the support we need to give all of our soldiers. To me, a good place to start is to stop calling them "troops." The work they have committed to requires that they put their humanity in a box. While soldiers must do this to survive the experience of war, I believe civilians share a responsibility to see that the humanity of soldiers is not lost completely. I also believe that many civilians are failing miserably in that regard, and have done so with veterans of past wars just as miserably.

Soldiers march into hell for us. They have volunteered to defend us with their lives, and it is up to us to watch their backs. It is easy to stand on the sidelines and criticize soldiers for their actions. We, as civilians, are just as much to blame for not giving soldiers a reason to retain their humanity. We have failed in our commitment to them. If we do not change course, we have lost a great deal more than lives on a battlefield. We need to believe in the good in humanity, in the good in those who serve to defend humanity, and in our responsibility to help preserve that humanity by opposing war with peace and a real respect for all life, not only the lives we choose to acknowledge.

I love my husband and my family—and I have worked hard and earned the right to respect myself. Knowing this, I will fight to preserve the good of humanity for them. They deserve that, and I believe I do as well. War should not be allowed to change everything.

October 2004—Stop-Loss

Monica Kevin was given stop-loss orders effective from October 2005 until May 2006. This was the last straw. He requested information about conscientious objection from a soldiers' resource organization that he then used to make his decision. When he first contacted the organization, he was told that the process could take up to eighteen months. Kevin considered a noncombat position instead of going through the process of a conscientious objector hearing because he knew he was scheduled to be discharged long before the process would have been completed. After the stop-loss order was issued he sought the paperwork to begin the conscientious objector process and tried repeatedly to meet with his battalion chaplain and company commander to get the interviews he needed to initiate the application. Neither officer would make himself available to assist Kevin as the army regulation demanded.

From this point on, the company commander began to make things very difficult for Kevin. He had Kevin working in the motor pool as well as handling his training room work. Kevin would leave for the night, and the captain was calling the house before Kevin even got home, wanting to know where the paperwork was that Kevin was to have completed. I would go back to the company with Kevin when he got home and the captain would be there with the paperwork in his hand and a sneer on his face.

One night we received a phone message for Kevin from the captain. He was very angry and used very abusive language. He was trying to get Kevin to come to the company to assist him in finding papers, but it was after Kevin had been released, and we were out with family. This message was left at nine o'clock at night. The company commander was repeatedly losing his control and was verbally abusive to soldiers in his company on many occasions.

It was at this time that the unit went to the rifle range for routine qualifications, and the company commander could not hit the targets. Finally, the first sergeant of the company spotted for the captain by lining up his sights so that he could then hit the target. The first sergeant later told Kevin to record that the captain had qualified even though every soldier in the unit knew that he had not. Kevin would not record the target, telling the first sergeant that he would have to do it. Several training reports were "pencil whipped" in this fashion; most were, actually. Kevin's command couldn't seem to get anything organized. Kevin reported some of this to the S-1, battalion training officer, who was in charge of personnel matters and who knew there were problems within the unit. The training officer who heard the complaints Kevin made would eventually be the rear detachment captain who would file the charges against Kevin. It didn't matter who the problems were reported to. Nothing was ever done. There were soldiers who reported their problems with the company commander to the division command sergeant major. That solved nothing. Even when the company commander was called and told by the division sergeant major that he needed to talk with his soldiers about concerns they were having, the company commander would not listen. This captain did not feel that he had to answer to any enlisted personnel and made that clear to everyone.

Five radios were lost from this unit at one point. These were sensitive pieces of equipment for which accountability should have been a priority. They could not be found, as the company commander had never assigned anyone to be responsible for them. When they were lost he held the unit responsible even though it was his bad management that caused the problem. This man learned his lessons well, following the example being set by the men who led him.

One night this unit was kept at company headquarters until midnight because the commander had lost one of his bags. He had left the company with it and the soldiers knew it. He threw one of his famous tantrums, yelling, swearing, and demanding that the soldiers locate his bag. He kept the entire unit there, including NCOs who were extremely angry for the way he threatened and berated the soldiers for his incompetence.

The company commander, first sergeant, and a circle of senior NCOs who seemed to believe their rank allowed them to disregard military regulations, did everything together. Every one of them disliked having to deal with their junior enlisted soldiers and took everything they could out on the younger men, directing absolute abuse at some of these soldiers. By the time of the deployment twelve were absent without leave (AWOL) that Kevin was aware of, all missing from deployment because the soldiers did not want to go to Iraq with these commanders. Even in Iraq the soldiers were taking abuse for the actions of these commanders. The younger soldiers were terrified of these men. One soldier finally stood up to his command to defend another younger soldier from the abuse he was being given. For doing what he could to protect the younger soldier, this specialist saw his leave form torn up and was not allowed to go on leave for his wedding. His wedding had to be canceled. The chain of command in this company was angry because this man stood up against them on behalf of a soldier suffering from PTSD who was not receiving any of the care he deserved.

3: Conscientious Objection

October 2004

Monica We began seeking guidance about conscientious objection from every avenue we could find. The counselor at the soldiers' rights organization was supportive and quick to respond to our questions regarding applications, how to file, and what the process would entail. We did a lot of our own research as well. We trusted ourselves most and wanted to see firsthand whether the information coming from others was accurate. This was Kevin's life, and the decision he made would affect him for the rest of his life. It was also a decision that would affect our family. This was not a decision to be made lightly, nor was it a decision that should be based on secondhand information. There are good people doing the work of peace, who do their best to present an unbiased truth, and we appreciate their support. Unfortunately this war has divided our country, and the divisions were evident to us as we researched conscientious objection. We found many people whose agendas were not to attend to the needs of an individual soldier with questions of conscience but rather to seek vengeance for the actions of an administration and to use the difficult situation soldiers found themselves in to achieve their goal. In many instances it seemed to us the vengeance had become very personal. We had to be careful, because this type of agenda could destroy someone caught up in its net.

It was autumn. When Kevin wasn't working with his unit, we took time to consider all the options available to us regarding Iraq, the army, and our future. The training grounds were not as busy these days, as soldiers were preparing for the possibility of returning to Iraq. They had been told that in January or February 2005 they would be ordered to deploy. Kevin's unit was still disorganized, and commanders were still not clear on who gave orders or how their soldiers were to complete the readiness process for an eventual deployment. From my perspective, the level of frustration that Kevin felt continued to grow, and I couldn't change what was happening. He tried to talk with the chaplain and with other members of the command. They seemed to have sensed his change in beliefs but did not want to address the issue. Kevin had several e-mail exchanges with his chaplain who was quite willing to discuss policy and what he felt soldiers should believe regarding war and their service. He was not willing to address Kevin's individual concerns to any extent, however, so we continued to seek advice on the best way to proceed.

One thing was clear from what I knew about Kevin: He was not going to do anything illegal to seek release from the military. He had served honorably for almost ten years. He had enlisted to defend the Constitution and the laws it represented. It would have violated his own standards and principles to break regulations to resolve the problems he was having in getting his command to fulfill its commitment to him and allow him the right to be released from further service as the regulations permitted.

This was a difficult time for me. I do not condone breaking the law to achieve desired results any more than Kevin does. It was clear from their actions that Kevin's commanders were hoping he would either break down and submit to their threats and intimidation or violate a regulation, giving them justification for further disciplinary action against him. I've learned that life can be far easier than most people seem to want to believe it to be. I tried living the hard way. I made costly mistakes in my life and paid a price to correct them. I've allowed others to pressure me into actions I was not comfortable with, regretting the actions later, but not as much as regretting their influence over me. After many years of listening to others who thought they knew, only to find out the hard way that they didn't, I came to realize it is best to listen to your conscience and do the right thing for yourself. It all works, and there is peace. What is the right thing? That is something to think about. Doing the right thing was something Kevin took a long time thinking about. It was something Kevin came to be willing to stand for and fight for in the most nonviolent manner he could.

I do not believe war or violence will ever achieve a positive result. It might prolong change, and it might set a range of policies in motion that give the illusion of positive change. But for me, nothing initiated by violent means can ever result in lasting good. People have argued with me that there have been just wars—the two world wars, for instance. But I don't see it. The peace and change that came after the world wars was not a result of war, but a result of people growing tired of war and working hard to see that policies for peace were implemented once the cease-fires were called. War is nothing but chaos. Peace comes when people have had enough of the chaos and are willing to make the sacrifices they must make to ensure that peace is restored. But the peace they restore never lasts. People have a short attention span and soon forget the horrendous acts of wartime, even forgetting to "support the soldiers" once the chaos settles down. In just a short time we find ourselves in a new conflict, and eventually in new efforts to end the conflict and restore peace. It always seems to take incredible pain before we are willing to make the sacrifices necessary to bring about a renewed sense of peace. It never seems that the hard lessons are learned, however.

What might happen if we simply made those sacrifices to begin with, without going through the chaos and destruction of war first?

• • •

The following article, "The Christmas Truce of 1914," by Robert Wilde, 2001, is from the About: European History Web site, http://europeanhistory.about.com/library/bldyk12.htm.

The Christmas Truce of 1914

Although the popular memory of World War One is normally one of horrific casualties and "wasted" life, the conflict does have tales of comradeship and peace. One of the most remarkable, and heavily mythologized, events concerns the "Christmas Truce" of 1914, in which the soldiers of the Western Front laid down their arms on Christmas Day and met in No Man's Land, exchanging food and cigarettes, as well as playing football. The cessation of violence was entirely unofficial and there had been no prior discussion: troops acted spontaneously from goodwill, not orders. Not only did this truce actually happen, but the event was more widespread than commonly portrayed.

There are many accounts of the Christmas truce, the most famous of which concern the meeting of British and German forces; however, French and Belgian troops also took part. The unofficial nature of the truce meant that there was no one single cause or origin; some narratives tell of British troops hearing their German counterparts singing Christmas carols and joining in, while Frank Richards, a private in the Royal Welsh Fusiliers, told of how both sides erected signs wishing the other a "Merry Christmas." From these small starts some men crossed the lines with their hands up, and troops from the opposing side went to meet them. By the time officers realized what was happening the initial meetings had been made, and most commanders either turned a blind eye or happily joined in.

The fraternization lasted, in many areas, for the whole of Christmas Day. Food and supplies were exchanged on a one-to-one basis, while in some areas men borrowed tools and equipment from the enemy, in order to quickly improve their own living conditions. Many games of football were played using whatever would suffice for a ball, while bodies that had become trapped within No Man's Land were buried.

Most modern retellings of the Truce finish with the soldiers returning to their trenches and then fighting again the next day, but in many areas the peace lasted much longer. Frank Richards's account explained how both sides refrained from shooting at each other the next day, until the British troops were relieved and they left the front line. In other areas the goodwill lasted for several weeks, bringing a halt to opportunistic sniping, before the bloody conflict once again resumed.

Kevin If these men could do this for one another during World War I, then why can't we do this for one another all the time? These men were able to remember their humanity during a war that took a huge toll on life, and they treated each other like friends and brothers for a period. If they can stop in the middle of a war and do this for each other, then it should be no problem for us to never start a war in the first place.

•   •   •

November 2004—Going Public

Monica This was the month when the soldiers began to pack their equipment for deployment. It was common knowledge that the company commander was still trying to receive definitive information about his company's assignment and how its deployment would be handled. He was still taking orders from both the 2-7th Infantry and 3rd Forward Support Battalion, and the orders made it very confusing and difficult for the soldiers in the company to know anything concrete about the coming months.

The main problem seemed to be that there was no organization as far as which company belonged to which battalion. The company was divided between the 2-7th Infantry and the 3rd Forward Support Battalion, and it took orders from both. This went on for the entire year. The soldiers received orders from one commander, then opposing orders from another commander. They didn't know where to requisition supplies, and they didn't know who their captain reported to. There were times when it didn't seem the captain cared if he reported to anyone; he created his own set of rules, regardless of the leadership.

At this point, Foxtrot Company still did not have everything it needed. The entire unit was one giant mess. Soldiers were not being taken care of, equipment was lacking, and morale was poor. Soldiers continued to report problems from this unit all the way to the command sergeant major of the division. He continued to listen, call the captain, and then drop the ball. Once the captain heard from the sergeant major that a soldier had reported problems, the captain would have the soldier disciplined by one of the senior NCOs who willingly kissed the captain's feet for a little special treatment.

Kevin spent the month of November trying to get an appointment to see the chaplain. He and the chaplain had an ongoing e-mail conversation, but it never went any further. Finally, at the end of November, Kevin wrote to the chaplain saying they still had not had a chance to talk in person about Kevin's concerns regarding war and his further participation in this one, and he wanted to arrange a meeting. This was when the chaplain replied with a statement that he was "not a yes-man" and that he loved to "mix it up with anybody." He said he would be happy to "debate" Kevin about his beliefs. This was not what Kevin wanted. Kevin wanted someone to give him some assistance in initiating his conscientious objector application.

• • •

November 20, 2004—Kevin's Letter to President George W. Bush

George Bush:

When are you going to tell the truth to the people of the United States? Why don't you tell them why you want to be in Iraq so bad? I was there for six months, and I did not see the first weapon of mass destruction. I did receive orders from the company commander to shoot children if they threw small rocks at us, and that was when I figured out that the entire thing was way over the line.

Over 1,200 soldiers have died in Iraq so that you can have a couple billion more dollars that should make you feel very good about yourself. The soldiers that have died for this sham that you have put over on the American people are so much more deserving than that. You are not worth the dust off of their boots. If you truly had respect for the military and the people that serve, then you would not continue to kill them in your war. I joined the army to protect my country and not to be a mercenary for a political despot. If you wish to put me in prison because of my views, then you should make room for about 75 percent of the military. And while you are at it, make some room for yourself and about half of your administration. You are responsible for what happened at Abu Ghraib and you are shirking your responsibility. The commander in chief is not above the UCMJ [Uniform Code of Military Justice], as you would like to believe.

I want to fulfill my contract that says I joined the army to protect my country against all enemies, foreign and domestic, and as far as I am concerned you are a domestic enemy of the United States. You care nothing for this country; you just care about the profits that are made from the oil in Iraq. That much is evident to me from the way the contracts were passed out to Halliburton and KBR. It must be nice to have the deck stacked in your favor by the president of the USA. Since you are raising the debt ceiling of America so that we can pay the bills that you have run up, why don't you forgive the debts of everyone in the armed forces, since they are the ones that are making it possible for you to make billions from the oil from Iraq.

SGT. Kevin M. Benderman

• • •

Kevin I had to say this to the man because I felt that no one else was calling him on his true intentions. I meant for this letter to be read by him only. I did not put it out for public consumption, and I am still not quite sure how it got out in the first place. But now that it is, I want everyone to know this is how I felt then, and this is how I still feel about it. The difference is that at this time there are almost 3,400 dead American service members, and God only knows how many Iraqis.

Monica Kevin and I spent a lot of time walking on the trails. We walked around ponds, through pine forests, and through hidden meadows far enough from the roadway to feel peaceful even in the middle of a military installation. After World War II the military decided to expand Fort Stewart. Several small communities were in the surrounding areas of the garrison, and when the military expansion was authorized, these small communities were taken over for training grounds. All that remain today are skeletons of houses, ancient orchards neatly lining what was once someone's proud homestead, and over three hundred tiny cemeteries scattered throughout the Georgia pine forests that are now part of a military installation.

We would drive across the trails in search of these cemeteries, park the truck under a tree, and walk around the headstones. Every marker told a story, and it gave us that much more to think about. Who were these people? What had they stood for? What had they felt when the military machine took away their homes? What would they want us to know today?

We walked through the remains of an abandoned house. We could touch the remnants of wallpaper and paint. We could feel the scratches on the mantelpiece and the cracks in the windowpanes. The boards of the front porch had rotted and fallen through, but it was easy to picture a time when things were different, when people met there on one of the sultry Georgia summer evenings and talked about the day's events. The yard was overgrown with wisteria and blackberry vines, but the old oak tree remained steadfast just off to one side of the porch, and there was surely a time when someone found the perfect spot to hide, sitting on one of its low-hanging limbs. People lived here. People died here. The military took over. Men and women were lost to a machine whose original purpose had been one of people committed to serving together to keep the peace and defend our freedoms, as outlined by our country's Constitution. Today, those serving still did so, believing they were to keep the peace and defend that same Constitution, but the machine had forgotten that it was the people who mattered. I was learning that firsthand. It made me angry and it made me realize, if we wanted to be remembered as human beings, we were going to have to see to it that we lived that way. I knew Kevin felt the same; I could see it by his actions and in the frustration he expressed at the way his command treated not only him but also the other soldiers he served with.

We received a call from the producer of a National Public Radio (NPR) program. He had heard that Kevin had been put on stop-loss and was speaking about his beliefs as a conscientious objector and as a veteran of the Iraq war. He wanted to interview Kevin about his feelings on stop-loss. We agreed. The interview aired, and the response was overwhelming.

Kevin found a Web site devoted to veterans' issues, in particular regarding the wars in Iraq and Afghanistan. Using the links available through the Web site, he posted a letter to the president (see the sidebar, "Kevin's Letter to President George W. Bush," p. 54). Army regulations allow soldiers the right to their political beliefs and the opportunity to express those beliefs as long as they are not in uniform or on duty. Kevin expressed his beliefs clearly.

We also began contacting attorneys to learn the legal steps for Kevin to take regarding discharge from the army. His command was absolutely not going to help. As a matter of fact, they were going to create as many stumbling blocks as possible to keep him from pursuing his legal right to conscientious objection.

Kevin The attorneys weren't much help; they wanted a $15,000 retainer up front before they would even begin to work on the case. Many of them like to pay lip service to helping soldiers, but when the truth is told, they are only concerned with the money. Don't get me wrong; I understand that the world operates on the almighty dollar, but sometimes you have to do the right thing regardless of the monetary gain or loss.

December 2004

Monica After months of research and a great deal of contemplation, it seemed that Kevin had decided applying for conscientious objector status was the right direction. If the commanders of Kevin's unit had acted with integrity, if soldiers were allowed to be released when their ETS date was scheduled, if stop-loss was not enacted, Kevin would have completed his ten years of service with an honorable discharge. He had been reassigned to a noncombat role, and with less than a year to serve, he would have left the military with a strong record of commitment, and we could have quietly moved on with our lives.

Unfortunately, the commanders had no intention of letting this happen. After they learned that Kevin had scheduled his ETS, they began a concerted effort to find justification for removing him from the position of training room NCO and returning him to the motor pool. They needed a mechanic of Kevin's caliber in the motor pool, but rather than admit this, they tried to discredit him in his other positions. As training room NCO, Kevin was also in a position to witness indiscretions in leadership from the chain of command. They became frustrated with the fact that he was not going to simply follow any orders without question, and he became a liability to their positions because of his outspokenness regarding their actions. They were failing in their leadership roles. Kevin and I were reaching the point where we had little tolerance for their egos or their attitudes toward the younger soldiers.

Kevin continued to seek meetings with the chaplain and company commander to no avail. He packed the bags he would be required to ship to Iraq in the conex boxes that would be sent along with the Bradleys and tanks.

I waited. I knew that I would support what Kevin chose to do, no matter what. I knew what I wanted him to decide and told him so. I also knew that Kevin would make up his own mind. If he didn't agree with me, he would choose as he felt best. I would either accept it or not, and the consequences of my choice would be my consequences. It had been that way between us from the start. We are both independent and have a tendency to march in the exact opposite direction of whatever anyone suggests for us. We knew that we could not influence each other to agree or disagree—we could only put our thoughts on the table and trust that we didn't weaken our relationship when we disagreed. I think the disagreements actually made it stronger. By our willingness to express our thoughts and feelings when we didn't agree, we reaffirmed our trust. It was easier for both of us to see truth in the differences than in the pleasant parts we shared. We had been caught off guard and taken advantage of too many times in the past by those who falsely claimed to understand. We have little trust for followers; they're not known for keeping their word. We hold on tightly to the fact that we are willing to tell each other the difficult truths when no one else will.

I was not happy with the idea that Kevin might have to return to Iraq, but there was nothing I could do about it. Whatever was coming was what we would have to get through. Before we were married, I had told him I was only doing this one more time, and if it wasn't something I could commit to for the duration, then I was not going to commit at all. I made the commitment; there was no going back, war or no war.

December 2004—Final Decisions

Monica The company went on block leave from December 1 to December 15. At this point, we had contacted attorneys for ways to approach the military about Kevin getting out because he was not getting any help from the military with regard to his conscientious objector application. We discussed stop-loss with them and illegality issues. Kevin was frustrated, and he wanted out. He had actually believed in the military until this command. He really felt that he could do something good for soldiers, and he was pretty demoralized when he realized that his command was not backing him up for all the honorable service he had given. What was worse, he could see what this command was doing to the other soldiers.

The chain of command, beginning with several of the platoon sergeants who catered to the higher-ranking officers, the first sergeant, and the company commander, all went to the bowling alley on post every day for lunch. They made the soldiers wait in formation by the company for two hours at a time while they were at the bowling alley, drinking and bowling during the daily lunch special. It was getting closer to deployment, and the soldiers were anxious to spend as much time as possible with their families. This company command showed how little respect there was for the men they were supposed to lead. Morale dipped lower and bad feelings festered long before the company left for Iraq. Soldiers did not trust the commanders as leaders because they were clearly not.

The company commander hated the fact that Kevin stood up for the soldiers. Kevin understood the regulations, he knew what it meant to lead, and he knew how much the younger soldiers needed a leader they could trust to be consistent.

A new soldier transferred from one unit to Kevin's company. He had been charged with driving under the influence (DUI) about six months before when he was with his former company. When he came to this one, the company commander ordered all the soldiers and NCOs to a DUI training session as a form of peer pressure against this soldier, but this soldier hadn't done anything during his time in this particular unit. There is a regulation that a soldier cannot be disciplined for something the soldier has not done. The NCOs in the unit did not attend the DUI weekend. This angered the company commander, but they all told him that if he wanted to discipline them, he would have to court-martial them all so that the real story would come out. He dropped the counseling statements, but the intimidation continued.

The company commander not only allowed his circle of officers and senior NCOs latitude in interpreting regulations regarding themselves, but he also disciplined those soldiers who stood by the rules, setting a standard he himself could not maintain. He was angry with Kevin because Kevin would not stay at the company till all hours of the night drinking with them and he would not go to the bowling alley with them. The captain told Kevin that personal family didn't matter. He wanted Kevin to believe the unit and the soldiers were Kevin's family, and he did not want Kevin leaving to come home at the end of the day. Kevin stood by his values and spent his free time with his family.

This just made the captain more determined to break Kevin. On numerous occasions the captain told Kevin and others that he hated all enlisted men. None of them were good. He also told Kevin that Kevin "had major balls to stand up to his company commander the way he did." He commented to several of the military wives that he did not respect them, he did not have to have anything to do with them, and he would not acknowledge them. When any of them tried to contact this man, even when he received an order from one of his superiors to do so, he did not follow through.

Things became more and more frustrating. It was becoming obvious there was no resolution other than conscientious objection, and we were getting very little cooperation from the command.

We had been speaking with members of an antiwar veterans' group about Kevin's situation. We had contacted members of the media about specific concerns Kevin had regarding company mismanagement, equipment issues, and the treatment of soldiers by the command.

I knew it was a difficult time for Kevin, more so than it was for me. Regardless of his decision, I was home and my life would have a semblance of continuity. Kevin was faced with difficult issues from many areas. He had already been to Iraq. His firsthand experiences had changed his beliefs about war, and no one seemed to care about

Kevin, the human being. Everything we were dealing with seemed to focus on legal issues, on contracts, and a sense of duty to others. Even those we spoke with in the media seemed more intent on the story they could write based on the facts Kevin shared with them, rather than how Kevin's experiences had changed the beliefs of a dedicated soldier. When would it come to be about the person, his human values, and his right to express them?

After months of listening to Kevin come home at night and talk about the inadequate leadership and mistreatment of the soldiers, I'd had enough. I wrote a five-page letter addressing many of the concerns we had regarding the lack of support we saw for the soldiers and the faulty leadership of a specific command. I wrote in general terms, using no names, but it was clear to those who knew them which command I was speaking of.

On December 22, 2004, my letter was first published on an alternative media site on the Internet. Kevin and I were not prepared for the number of responses we received or their overwhelmingly supportive messages.

This made our situation even more difficult. It would be wrong to allow the steady support we began to receive from people around the world to have too much influence over how we decided to proceed. It was important that we continue to look for the best solution for Kevin and to pursue his goal of a legal, honorable discharge from the military service that his beliefs and principles no longer agreed with. We had to be certain that neither the actions of the military nor the actions of those who were now sending their support to us compromised the clarity with which we made the decisions that were best for us.

December 15 – 31, 2004

Monica Every day, Kevin tried to get someone in the command to talk with him about his conscientious objector application. No one would, and the battalion chaplain had turned off his phone. Finally, on December 28, Kevin placed a DA Form 4187 (Department of the Army change of status request) in the company commander's box, because he would not accept it in person. We also e-mailed the finished five-page conscientious objector application to the chaplain so someone would see that it had been turned in. We e-mailed this on December 30 and e-mailed it again on January 7, because the chaplain said he knew nothing about it.

The captain called Kevin into his office on the morning of December 30 and told him that he would not allow Kevin to file for conscientious objector status, and he returned the DA Form 4187 signed by him in the space marked "recommend disapproval." He told Kevin that if he could find someone else to help him with it, he could not stop it, but that he was not going to assist Kevin in any way. This is against Army Regulation 600-43, the regulation that governs conscientious objection.

Kevin went to his first sergeant for help. The first sergeant called Kevin a coward, told him that he *would* be going to Iraq, and that no one was going to help him. Kevin went to the battalion command sergeant major. The sergeant major told Kevin that he would not help him. Kevin was on his own. He asked Kevin if he knew why we were in Iraq. The sergeant major told Kevin they were going to Iraq to kill people who were raping eight-year-old children.

The sergeant major told Kevin that if he followed through with his application, he would be reassigned to a place somewhere out in the middle of the desert. He said that it would be surrounded by Bradleys, that it was where all the conscientious objector applicants were stationed in Iraq. He said that it was a "support base," and there was a clear view for miles in case of enemy approach. He told Kevin not to worry about being there, because if the enemy did approach, the enemy would throw their grenades or launch their missiles, but none would reach the base itself. The grenades would simply bounce off the Bradleys surrounding them, and the enemy would move off. Kevin's command ordered him not to speak about his conscientious objector application with any of the other soldiers in his unit.

We contacted our congressional representative after the last wall was put up. Kevin tried to find another chaplain, but he was told that he needed to see his battalion chaplain. Kevin tried to go to the Division of Mental Health, another requirement for the conscientious objector application process. He made an appointment, but once he got there he was told that he could not be seen by anyone without approval from his company commander, who was not going to cooperate in any way.

We sent all the paperwork we had to the congressional office for review.

December 25, 2004

Monica Kevin's company had several days off for the holidays. There was still no definite date for deployment other than the company being told that it would most likely be the week of January 12, 2005. We had been through this before. In the military you learn to be prepared for anything, at any time, with no warning.

We spent the holidays quietly. We continued to receive hundreds of e-mails of support for the letter I had written. The support was appreciated, but it really did not solve the problem. People were hearing the truth we presented, but we had the sense that they wanted more, for the truth to be used in a way we had not intended. We were immersed in reality, and reality was enough for us. It was time for people to recognize reality for what it was, to stop the hyperbole and dramatization. We were concerned that their interpretations of our message would interfere with the message we wanted to convey. Since the time Kevin spent in Iraq, we had been doing what we could to get help for the enlisted soldiers who were faced with commanders who seemed to have little accountability to anyone but themselves. Since Iraq, Kevin had been concerned with the lack of supplies, the lack of adherence to the rules of war, the lack of real leadership from the officers in command, the lack of quality equipment, and the lack of concern for the situation the soldiers were now in. There were political issues this country was eventually going to have to deal with, but for us, the first priority was ensuring that the real needs of the soldiers were met. Many people spoke of being in agreement with our position, but few actually acted in a manner that showed any kind of commitment behind their words. Reality, it seems, was destined to be lost in the overdramatization so many believed necessary to defend their positions and attain the publicity they craved. We wanted a straightforward discussion of the needs of soldiers and their families, real people, and a defined, realistic solution to what they faced on a daily basis, something civilian participants in an overhyped "peace movement" and government leadership continually overlooked.

December 30, 2004

Monica Kevin submitted a form to his company commander requesting that the captain accept Kevin's conscientious objector application and begin the process of administering it as army regulations dictated. The captain had been very uncooperative for almost three months in regard to Kevin's concerns. It was no different now. Ultimately, in violation of the army regulation for conscientious objection, the captain returned Kevin's request: denied.

This just made the frustration level that much higher. I could see the emotions building in Kevin. He is strong, and normally those emotions are well controlled. Control became more difficult for him, and I understood.

During the week that followed the captain's denial of Kevin's request, Kevin did everything he could to find one officer in his brigade who was willing to help him. He was unrelenting even when his superiors called him a coward, threatened him with loss of security clearance, menial tasks in Iraq, and a myriad of other intimidations.

There was nothing I could do except support him by listening and ensuring a measure of normalcy at home. He continued to think through his situation. The kids and animals did what they could to offer an occasional diversion, but time was essential now, and it seemed that the command was doing everything it could to make things as difficult as possible for Kevin.

Even those we sought for advice had little of real substance to offer. The ideas were there, but we learned quickly—the military had been at this for a very long time. Ideas were fruitless without action behind them. There was little precedent for standing by the regulations while simultaneously adhering to personal standards of conscience against the military. The response we found from those who offered advice was break a law, violate a regulation, run. Kevin and I had learned from years of hard lessons, you don't solve problems by running from them. They eventually catch up with you. What was needed seemed to be the creation of greater public awareness of the type of control officers were able to have over their soldiers. It required public attention for the fact that some officers and senior NCOs were willing to go so far as to manipulate documents, misinterpret regulations, and use threats and intimidation to bring an independent-thinking soldier back into their control. The regulations were there, but with little accountability to the outside world, commanders had a great deal of latitude in the threats and mistreatment they could mete out to their soldiers, even if it meant violating regulations. The command was willing to break regulations; Kevin was not. In the world of military justice, regardless of the regulations, it became the word of the officer against that of the enlisted soldier. A weak officer was willing to manipulate any situation to gain the advantage, and the enlisted soldier had to be incredibly strong and sure of the truth to continue to stand against the threats and abuse of this kind of command.

January 2005

Monica At this point, the soldiers still had not been given a definite date for deployment, but they knew it was sometime in the first two weeks of the new year. Kevin had been told that he might deploy on the fifth, but that came and went with no one saying anything to him. He was then told that it looked like they would be deploying from the fifth to the twelfth, but he was never given a specific time or a date. He was never shown a manifest.

We had again been in contact with the producer of an NPR program who had been following Kevin's situation and what now appeared to him to be a developing story. We spoke with the studio almost daily, giving updates to the events surrounding the deployment, Kevin's concern regarding the lack of attention to his conscientious objector application, and discussing our feelings over what was happening.

It was an uncomfortable feeling for Kevin and me. Neither one of us are public people. I prefer to simply do whatever is necessary to keep myself moving forward and to keep my life centered. I don't like conflict, and I will work hard to find a solution when faced with having to deal with conflict. There is always a mature, calm way to handle any situation, in my opinion—something I learned after many years of fruitlessly believing I could change a situation simply by being the one with the loudest demand for change. People should be willing to sit across from each other and respect their different perspectives. Rather than forcibly trying to control the actions of another, wouldn't it be better to learn who they are by learning to control ourselves, allowing others to learn to do the same, and sharing our differences in a reasonable discussion?

The key to a strong military, according to statements made by many officers, is to enforce good discipline over the soldiers, essentially to control their actions so that they fall in line with the wishes of the command. Kevin's command was corrupt, and Kevin stood firm in expecting it to follow the regulations and take care of the unit's soldiers. We did not want public attention. It came to a point, however, where it seemed that the army gave Kevin no other choice.

We had seen the mistreatment of many soldiers in the course of the year leading to this second deployment. Soldiers who needed counseling were brushed off. Soldiers who had problems within their families as a result of their previous deployment were not given the support they needed. Soldiers in financial trouble were disciplined but not given assistance in working out their problems. Kevin wanted to help them all, but one NCO in a company with an unsupportive command element wasn't enough. There were other NCOs equally concerned but less willing to speak up against the command. Threats were common in this unit, and many of the NCOs had much younger families to consider. Sadly, this played into the hands of the commanders, as they used whatever means at their disposal to ensure the outward appearance of a battle-ready company that in reality was steeped in low morale.

In our discussions with others, it became clear that there was very little anyone was able to do. Most people who had faced problems in the military in the past had run from them or resigned themselves to the fact that the army would win. That just frustrated us all the more. People would write and tell us that Kevin had volunteered for the army; he should have known what it was like. Former military people would tell him to finish his time and move on. All that meant to us was this command would continue its corrupt practices knowing it would not be held accountable for violating the very regulations it had sworn to uphold.

January 6, 2005

Monica Since turning in his conscientious objector application, Kevin's chain of command had put up every wall possible to prevent him from receiving the due process military regulations allowed. When Kevin went to work, he was called into a counseling session by his company commander. This was clearly the captain's latest attempt at intimidating Kevin. He called every senior NCO from the company, along with three lieutenants, into his office to witness his "dressing down" of Kevin. Later, in testimony during the Article 32 hearing, which is something like a preliminary hearing or a discovery hearing in civilian terms, all three lieutenants testified that they thought it quite strange for the commander to have done this. All three also testified that at no time did the captain mention the Iraq deployment nor Kevin's status in reference to it.

The captain made several threats against Kevin, his rank, and his future service during this counseling session. He taped the entire event but later denied knowing where the tape was. The captain was clearly angry that Kevin had filed a conscientious objector application and was even more disturbed by the letter I had published on the Web site in December. We both found this to be telling. I had not made any specific mention of any officer or soldier when writing about our concerns over situations at Fort Stewart, in particular with one unit. The captain was angry because we had found a way to bring attention to the intimidation, threats, and incompetence many soldiers had tried to report through the chain of command for almost a year, with no positive result. This was a weak captain and his guilt was showing through his actions.

The captain threatened Kevin with two charges of violating the Uniform Code of Military Justice (UCMJ); "making disloyal statements" and "disrespecting a superior officer." It was clear this commander was coming unhinged and would do whatever he could to punish Kevin for standing up to him. There was no justification for either charge, which is what a judge advocate general (JAG) officer explained to the commander after the meeting was adjourned.

It had become clear that Kevin was going to need assistance with his conscientious objector application from an authority outside the military command. We called our congressional representative, who was more than willing to assist. She prepared a strong letter of support, urging Kevin's chain of command to seriously consider placing Kevin in the rear detachment and to process his conscientious objector application. This letter was faxed to several members of the command on the morning of January 7. The congresswoman's office stayed in contact with us, and notified us that there had been an acknowledgment of receipt of her fax.

I continued to believe that the command would come to its senses. With the level of public pressure Kevin's commanders were now receiving, they would certainly realize the sense in following regulations. Kevin wasn't so sure. He continued to prepare for an eventual deployment order, packing last-minute supplies and tying up loose ends around the house.

It would be wrong to say we weren't concerned about the whole situation, but it would also be wrong to say we didn't feel calm. The worst that would happen was that Kevin would return to another tour in Iraq. We'd been through that before. We'd both been through the anger, frustration, and grief—emotions I think all soldiers and their families were feeling at the thought of returning to a war that was becoming increasingly more destructive and uncontrolled. We had expressed every range of emotion we felt during the course of the last year leading up to these last few days. Having gotten through all of that, it had now become a matter of moving forward and getting through whatever was yet to come. It was no different than the first deployment, except this time the soldiers in Kevin's unit would be serving with a chain of command that didn't have the first clue about how to lead.

January 7, 2005

Monica Kevin's company had been ordered to report to the company headquarters for a formation at 1500 hours. We'd been through this before as well. During the first deployment, soldiers were ordered to formations repeatedly only to be told deployment plans had changed. Kevin spent the morning working on some minor household repairs, leaving for a short time to purchase some supplies. While he was gone, the first sergeant of his company called to speak with him. I took a message that Kevin was to call as soon as he returned, which he did. The first sergeant informed Kevin that he was not to go to the 1500 formation as ordered. Kevin was ordered to attend a meeting with the command sergeant major of the battalion during that time instead; a meeting we learned during courtroom testimony had been arranged by the battalion commander.

At 1500 hours Kevin and I were at the office of the command sergeant major waiting for him to arrive. There was a lot of activity at the battalion headquarters, but we could not find the sergeant major. After waiting for several minutes, we found the battalion commander, a lieutenant colonel, who clearly informed Kevin that the sergeant major was not available for the 1500 meeting, but the meeting had been rescheduled for 1700 hours that evening. Kevin was excused by the battalion commander until the 1700 meeting with the sergeant major. We left the installation and returned home. We had heard from our congresswoman's office that the fax she had sent had been received by the battalion commander. We had also received a copy of the fax, and it had been addressed not only to the battalion commander, but also the command sergeant major. We were quite hopeful, with events happening as they had been, that the congresswoman's recommendations had been received and were being sensibly acted on by the command.

We arrived about ten minutes early for the rescheduled meeting with the sergeant major. Once again we found ourselves waiting outside his office. This time he appeared, and after a quick introduction, I remained in a chair outside his office while he and Kevin went inside. As the door closed I could hear the sergeant major read Kevin his rights from a rights card he had in his hand. I also heard Kevin ask if he was being charged with anything, as the meeting of the day before, in which his company commander threatened him with criminal charges, was still fresh in both our minds. The sergeant major assured Kevin there were no charges; he was only reading Kevin his rights as a precaution. The games of the command continued.

I could hear bits and pieces of what was said between Kevin and the sergeant major. Kevin invoked his rights and refused to answer any of the ensuing questions asked by the sergeant major. This appeared to frustrate the sergeant major. He wanted Kevin to talk to him about the company and the actions of the command. He said that he was certain it was the actions of the command that had caused Kevin to file a conscientious objector application. Kevin had invoked his rights. He would not answer the questions. After this had gone on for several minutes, the sergeant major suggested that they make the conversation informal. He would simply like to talk to Kevin about the conditions within the company, man to man—"Sam to Kevin"—off the record.

Twenty-five minutes had passed when Kevin opened the door and asked me to join them in the office. The sergeant major appeared uncomfortable, unsure of himself. He made some sexist comments to Kevin in reference to my appearance. Kevin stood at ease next to the desk and said nothing. I sat down. The sergeant major then explained that he had written a statement saying that Kevin had refused to deploy, Kevin would not sign the paper, and the sergeant major needed a witness. I looked at Kevin, asking him if he thought I should sign it. He responded that I should do what I thought and said nothing more. The sergeant major had drawn a line at the bottom of the hand-written words on the page, and beneath it, he had written "witnes" [*sic*]. I told him that I could not be a witness because I was not in the room for the conversation, and Kevin was my husband. He said he didn't want a witness to what was said; he wanted a witness to what was written. That made absolutely no sense to me and I said so. After a few minutes of thinking about the best course of action, I realized that it might be best to sign to keep from having anything further written. It would not be admissible anyway. I signed, dated it, and also put the time: 1738.

I then asked the sergeant major if he would mind if I asked him a few questions, civilian to civilian. He seemed to have no problem with that, and with Kevin standing at ease by the desk, I began a conversation, asking the sergeant major how he felt about war and killing, whether he had ever killed anyone, and if so, what it felt like.

We discussed conscientious objection, his beliefs and his experiences with conscientious objectors, and even his childhood. Kevin requested permission to leave the room to make a copy of what I had signed, which was granted. When Kevin returned, the sergeant major asked Kevin several times if he really wanted to go through with his conscientious objector application. Kevin replied in the affirmative each time. The sergeant major reminded Kevin that the process would be a difficult one, and time-consuming. He stated that Kevin would face questions from many commanders, hearings regarding his beliefs, and would have a great deal of paperwork. He went on to say that he would take Kevin's application and toss it in the trash and forget the entire conversation if Kevin had any second thoughts. Kevin said he understood, but that he wanted to submit his application and have it given the respect it deserved. The sergeant major suggested that Kevin should begin work immediately on the process. When Kevin asked if he was released to do this, the sergeant major confirmed the order. Kevin repeated the request two more times before he was certain that was what the sergeant major was ordering him to do. Kevin looked at me, the sergeant major wished Kevin good luck, and we walked out of the office.

Outside the office was a small conference room. As we walked past the room we could see Kevin's company commander sitting inside with his wife and a child in a stroller. There was no acknowledgment from the captain, simply a blank stare. We walked past the room, Kevin signed out with the same staff duty sergeant he had signed in with an hour before, and we drove home. That was the last we heard from anyone in Kevin's company until two days later, when Kevin was called to report to the rear detachment unit for formation on Monday morning.

We did receive a phone message from the wife of a soldier in Kevin's unit. When we returned home from the meeting with the sergeant major, I checked for messages, and she had left one shortly before we arrived home. She was distraught and needed help. Her husband had attempted suicide that morning and the company commander was angry, uncooperative, and making things very difficult for her. She knew Kevin had been standing up for the soldiers against the threats and intimidation of the company commander. She was hoping that I would be able to help her with her husband's situation. She was not aware of the meeting we had had with the sergeant major, and hadn't anticipated that Kevin would be home. She was calling to ask me for help. I told her we would both do what we could to help. Kevin had been released after the meeting, he was an NCO who cared about the soldiers in his unit, and he was familiar with what they had all been through.

Kevin This entire meeting with the command sergeant major was bizarre. The first thing he did was read the rights warning from a card he had. I invoked my Article 31 rights under the UCMJ (the same as the 5th Amendment to the Constitution), and the man proceeded to question me anyway. This is in direct violation of military regulations and the UCMJ.

The man told me he wanted to talk just "Sam to Kevin," with no rank involved or anything being official—off the record, so to speak. He asked what was wrong with my command that would make me file for conscientious objection. I had invoked my rights so I did not say anything, and yet he persisted. He asked what I would do if I was ordered to fly out to Iraq as a hypothetical question, and so I gave him a hypothetical answer. I told him at that point, I guessed I would refuse.

The man reacted as if I had just slapped his momma; he got all flustered and said that he would have to write a sworn statement, which is a DA Form 2823. At first he did not even know the correct form to use, and asked me what it was. I told him which one to use, and he tried to use a computer to generate the form, but apparently he lacked computer skills, so he did it by hand. He then wanted me to sign it as a witness, which I would not do. He apparently did not think to get the staff duty NCO to sign the thing, so he asked my wife to sign it, which she did at 1738 hours on January 7, 2005.

After this had transpired and my wife had spoken with him for a few minutes, he leaned back in the chair and said, "I guess that's it then." He then proceeded to tell me that I needed to work on my conscientious objector packet. I asked him if I was released to do this and he replied in the affirmative. I confirmed this two more times before I left his office with Monica.

January 8, 2005

Monica Kevin and I went shopping at the commissary on post this morning. We were on post for about two hours.

We spent this day going back and forth with the wife of the specialist who had attempted suicide, doing everything we could to get her help to see her husband and to see that he received the care he should. Two soldiers from this battalion were in the psychiatric unit and had received treatment for suicide. Not one but two specialists from the battalion were being treated. The first, whose wife had come to us, had taken thirty-two Percocet tablets in his bathroom. The second specialist had reportedly driven to Highway 16 out beyond Fort Stewart, parked alongside the road, and taken an overdose of prescription medications, gotten out of his car, and walked away from it with a loaded gun. Fortunately, he passed out before he could use the gun. He was deployed about a week after his suicide attempt. The first specialist went AWOL four days after his attempt.

Kevin The young specialist whose wife contacted us for help was treated very badly by the command element of this company. This soldier had gone to Iraq and served a combat tour. The things this young man had seen while there had a very adverse affect on him. He attempted suicide as a result, and instead of the command taking care of this soldier like they wanted everyone to believe they were, they berated him and his wife.

The soldier had been taken to the nearby civilian medical center where he was receiving treatment for an overdose of painkillers. When the commanders found out where he was, they proceeded to force the medical center to release this soldier against its judgment. When the command had this soldier transferred to the army hospital on Fort Stewart, it began to threaten this young soldier and his wife.

He was told that if he did not stop "malingering," he would be sent to Iraq in his hospital pajamas and with leg-irons and handcuffs. When his wife tried to see him in the hospital room, the commander physically shoved her out of the room and proceeded to yell and shout at the soldier.

This command was entirely out of control and on a very serious power trip. These people should be held accountable for what they did, and if I have a say in the matter, they will be. I have not forgotten the way they treated everyone in their company in general and some in particular. I am going to continue to push the appropriate people to hold these people accountable for what they did to soldiers.

This is only one example of the way they treated soldiers in their command.

January 9, 2005

Monica Kevin worked on additional info for his conscientious objector packet all weekend, including a statement of why he was filing for conscientious objector status.

On this evening Kevin received a call from a staff sergeant in rear detachment telling him to report for duty at 9 a.m. on January 10 in BDUs. Kevin spoke with this staff sergeant about the order, and we went to bed.

Kevin When I received the call from the rear detachment NCO and was told to report to the rear detachment formation on Monday, January 10, 2005, I figured I was to be officially signed into the rear detachment while the conscientious objector packet was completed and then submitted through the proper channels. Little did I know what they had planned at that time.

The rear detachment commander was in Louisiana at a dedication ceremony celebrating the anniversary of the 2-7th Infantry. This individual was not present when I talked to the command sergeant major, or anyone else, and yet he felt as though he had enough "evidence" to press charges against me for desertion and missing movement. How this can be done on hearsay is beyond my ability to understand, but knowing how this command element operates as well as I do, it wasn't a real surprise.

They also were going to issue an order for me to fly out on January 12, 2005, as noted in a sworn statement written by the company commander from Kuwait on January 9, but somehow they managed to forget to do this and filed charges instead. There was much confusion from everyone involved. The JAG officer they consulted talked to me and apparently did not feel as if they had a case; he wished me good luck as he was leaving to be deployed to Iraq. The rear detachment commander and the prosecuting attorneys cooked up a harebrained idea to issue an order for me to deploy while they were prosecuting me for missing movement. They even put this stupidity into writing in the form of a counseling statement. The amazing thing is that this was the prosecuting attorneys' idea, because they knew they had no real evidence against me and they were trying to come up with anything they could to use against me. The entire thing is pathetically funny because these idiots are in the U.S. Army and are charged with protecting the laws of the land.

January 10, 2005

Monica The next morning, Kevin went to formation as ordered, taking an additional copy of his conscientious objector packet and the added information with him. After reporting in, he was told that he was to be questioned by a major who served as the brigade legal advisor, along with the rear detachment commander, and he was to wait for that meeting. These two never showed up, so Kevin asked the staff sergeant on duty if he could go to the division inspector general's office. He wanted to report the problems we had encountered with the specialist and his wife over the weekend. Kevin was released, and he spent most of the afternoon trying to get someone in the inspector general's office to take a statement about the younger soldier. The specialist's wife also showed up, along with another soldier's wife and a sergeant from Kevin's rear detachment unit, all of whom were aware of the problems within the unit and those that directly related to this young specialist. This sergeant was on rear detachment because of leg surgery and was in a cast. No one from the inspector general's office would take a written statement.

The injured sergeant was assigned to watch the soldier who had attempted suicide, and the soldier was allowed out of the psychiatric unit for a visit with his kids. The soldier had other plans, however, and once released from the psychiatric unit, he managed to evade those watching him, and he was gone. He remained AWOL for about two weeks. This family had its own battle with the same company commanders that sought to prosecute Kevin. Many soldiers had to deal with threats, intimidation, and more because of the incompetence and lack of integrity within this command.

At this point, two more flights were leaving for Iraq. The last flight scheduled was on January 12. In a sworn statement written the day after Kevin met with his sergeant major, the company commander had stated that he had left word with rear detachment that Kevin was to be ordered to fly on the plane leaving on January 12.

Kevin was officially placed in rear detachment on January 11. Kevin was never given an order to fly by any officer on any plane scheduled.

Kevin's rear detachment commander was in Louisiana during the time that all of these events took place. He did not return to Fort Stewart until January 10.

Both the company commander and the command sergeant major sent sworn statements from Kuwait outlining their perception of what had happened during the last four days. Their statements were conflicting, and later on in the course of preparing for the court-martial, it became clear that they were both unreliable. They offered several sworn statements over the duration of the proceedings that not only conflicted with each other's perceptions of the facts, but also with their own as well.

January 11, 2005

Monica Kevin was reassigned to rear detachment. The command accepted his conscientious objector application, and the process of evaluating it began. We were prepared for this to take the remainder of the year, possibly longer. All accounts confirmed it to be a long, drawn-out process. Kevin was given a mental health evaluation, and he was interviewed by a major who was serving as a division chaplain. After the interview this major wrote a very strong letter on Kevin's behalf, attesting to Kevin's sincerity in his conscientious objector beliefs.

Kevin was read his rights on five different occasions by five different people.

In addition to an investigation into whether they could bring charges against Kevin and have him court-martialed, an investigative hearing was being scheduled for his conscientious objector application.

January 18, 2005

Monica Kevin was charged with "Missing Movement by Design, and Desertion with the Intent to Avoid Hazardous Duty."

The Article 32 hearing, which would determine if Kevin would be court-martialed, was scheduled for February 7, 2005, and the conscientious objector hearing was scheduled for February 8, 2005.

Kevin's defense attorney filed motions requesting that the lieutenant colonel who had been assigned as the investigating officer for the Article 32 hearing be recused because of potential conflicts with her past service and her working relationship with the detailed (assigned) military defense attorney. These motions were denied.

Kevin's defense attorney filed a request for a delay in the conscientious objector hearing with the captain who had been assigned as investigating officer for the hearing, a military intelligence officer for the 2-7th Infantry. He also asked that this officer be recused because of his relationship with the same unit that Kevin was in, and because he was acquainted with the command of Kevin's unit. This also was denied.

On this date the rear detachment command gave Kevin a list of questions that related to problems within the command that Kevin dealt with. He asked Kevin to answer the questions in spite of the fact that Kevin had already been read his rights five different times and was represented by defense counsel. He asked Kevin to fill out another sworn statement about why he "refused to deploy," which was not only leading but inappropriate now that Kevin had legal representation. Kevin did not answer the questions. There was a lot going on at this time. Kevin's commanders applied a lot of pressure, and it was clear they were trying to shake Kevin's confidence with everything happening at once.

• • •

A Matter of Conscience—
Sgt. Kevin Benderman

Having watched and observed life from the standpoint of a soldier for ten years of my life, I always felt there was no higher honor than to serve my country and defend the values that established it. My family has a history of serving this country dating from the American Revolution, and I felt that to continue on in that tradition was the honorable thing to do.

As I went through the process that led to my decision to refuse deployment to Iraq for the second time, I was torn between thoughts of abandoning the soldiers that I serve with or following my conscience, which tells me that war is the ultimate in destruction and a waste of humanity.

Thoughts that we could, and should, consider better ways to solve our differences with other people in the world have crossed my mind on numerous occasions. And this was the driving force that made me refuse deployment to Iraq for a second time. Some people may say I am doing so out of fear of combat; I am not going to tell you that the thought of going back to that place isn't scary, but that is not the reason for my decision to not return.

I want people to know that the longer I thought about just how stupid the concept of war really is, the stronger I felt about not participating in war. Why do we tell our children to not solve their differences with violence, then turn around and commit the ultimate in violence against people in another country who have nothing to do with the political attitudes of their leaders?

Having read numerous books on the subject of war and having heard all the arguments for war, I have come to the conclusion that there are no valid arguments for the destructive force of war. People are destroyed, nations are destroyed, and yet we continue on with war. The young people I went with to the combat zone looked at it like it was a video game they played back in their childhood.

When you contemplate the beauty of the world around us and the gifts we have been given, you have to ask yourself, "Is this what humanity is meant to do—wage war against one another?"

Why can't we teach our children not to hate or to not be afraid of someone else just because the person is different from us? Why must it be considered honorable to train young men and women to look through the sights of a high-powered rifle and to kill another human being from three hundred meters away?

Consider, if you will, the positive things that could be accomplished without war in our lives: prescription medication that is affordable for seniors, college grants that are available for high school seniors—I could make a list of reasons not to waste our resources on war. The most important being to let the children of the world learn war no more.

I've received e-mails from people who said that I was a coward for not going to war, but I say to them that I have already been, so I do not have anything to prove to anyone anymore. What is there to prove anyway—that I can kill someone I do not even know and who has never done anything to me? What is in that concept that anyone could consider honorable?

I first realized that war was the wrong way to handle things in this or any other country when I went to the war zone and saw the damage that it causes. Why must we resort to violence when things do not go our way? Where is the logic of that? I have felt that there are better ways to handle our business than to bomb each other into oblivion. When you are on the water in a boat and you have a chance to see dolphins playing with each other as they go about their business, you realize that if they can live without war, then humanity should be able to as well.

Can't we teach our children to leave war behind in history where it belongs? We realized that slavery and human sacrifice were obsolete institutions, and we left them behind us. When are we going to have the same enlightened attitude about war?

I look at my stepchildren and realize that war has no place with me in giving them what they need to survive the trials and tribulations of early adulthood. And if you look at all the time soldiers lose in the course of fighting wars, such as birthdays and anniversaries, their children going to the senior prom and college graduations, and other things that can never be replaced, then you have to come to the understanding that war steals more from people than just the sense of humanity—it also steals some of that humanity from their family.

I have learned from firsthand experience that war is the destroyer of everything that is good in the world; it turns our young into soulless killers, and we tell them that they are heroes when they master the "art" of killing. That is a very deranged mind-set in my opinion. It destroys the environment, life, and the resources that could be used to create more life by advancing our endeavors.

War should be left behind us; we should evolve to a higher mind-set even if it means going against what most people tell us in this country, such as the idea that we can never stop fighting with other people in the world. I have made the decision to not participate in war any longer, and while some people in this country cannot comprehend that concept, to me it is simple. I have chosen not to take part in war, and it was easy to come to that decision.

I cannot tell anyone else how to live his or her life, but I have determined how I want to live mine—by not participating in war any longer, as I feel that it is stupid and against everything that is good about our world.

• • •

January 2005

Monica This was quite a month. I felt as if I were being pulled uncontrollably along in a current and soon came to believe the best solution was to take it one step at a time. I had learned to have no expectations, especially when it came to the army. If I thought a situation would move in one direction, chances were it would go in exactly the opposite. It seemed to become a game to those in command here. They had already broken regulations and in the process had lost sight of the truth. Well, perhaps not so much lost sight of it as made a choice to cover it up. After putting themselves in the position of having to create a story to protect their incompetence, they could no longer admit the truth, so it became a mind game to them. Kevin's refusal to further participate in this war was a legal refusal offered by way of his conscientious objector application, but the army claimed he refused an order. Could they manipulate events, issues, and the situation enough so that Kevin became less sure of what he knew to be true, and could they influence me in the same manner to help them regain control of this soldier? In truth, no.

February 7, 2005

Monica This was the date of the Article 32 hearing. Little to no evidence was presented that could firmly support the charges filed against Kevin. When the hearing was completed, no verbatim transcripts were prepared. The summarized transcripts were created from the recorded testimony by a specialist assigned to the JAG office, and the decision in Kevin's case about whether to proceed to court-martial depended on the accuracy of this testimony. The testimony was summarized, and the summary was at the discretion of an army specialist or private easily intimidated by those of a higher rank with reason to influence the outcome of a court-martial.

Here we had a man's career—and his life—at stake, not to mention the life of his family. The actions of this group of army officers demonstrated how little regard they had for the humanity of their soldiers.

All prosecution witnesses who were involved in the January 6 counseling session and the events of January 7 through January 10 were in Iraq. None of them were returned to Fort Stewart for the hearing. They all testified telephonically, and they were all in the room at the same time. There was no space between the testimonies while the next person was brought in; the phone stayed on, and it was just passed along to the next person in the room to be called to testify.

The only prosecution witnesses to testify from Fort Stewart were in the rear detachment command. The captain of the rear detachment is the commander who brought the charges against Kevin, and yet he was not even in the state on the days in question. He had nothing to do with any of the events in question. It was all through testimony presented in statements from the forward company commander, command sergeant major, and first sergeant that he made his decision.

Their statements changed several times over the course of the investigation and ensuing court-martial process.

No witnesses were presented at this time for the defense.

February 8, 2005

Monica The request for an extension of the conscientious objector hearing was denied. The hearing officer stated that there was nothing Kevin needed to prepare for in spite of the fact that his Article 32 hearing was scheduled the day before. But in his recommendation, the hearing officer stated that justification for his recommendation of denial of Kevin's application was based on Kevin not being prepared for the hearing.

On February 7 we received a call from a local Savannah news reporter who had been covering the entire situation since the beginning of January. He asked if we had requested that the conscientious objector hearing be closed. He had gone to the Army Public Affairs Office to find out the particulars of the hearing. The public affairs officer (PAO) told this reporter the hearing was to be closed. Kevin was surprised at this and informed the reporter it was not to be closed; he wanted witnesses. The reporter required the services of the newspaper's attorney to make this happen. When he pressured the PAO's office, the staff not only gave him and his attorney the wrong time but also the wrong location for the hearing. Even on the morning of the hearing, the PAO's office was still giving them a hard time about the hearing. Finally, the reporter did get there, about forty-five minutes late.

Kevin's military defense attorney and I were present at the hearing, along with the appointed hearing officer and the PAO.

The hearing officer, in a series of e-mail exchanges with Kevin's defense attorney, had stated that Kevin did not need to provide a court reporter for this hearing as the military would provide one. At the outset of the hearing, the investigating officer admitted that he had just learned that he was not responsible for providing a court reporter, and for the first time also admitted that he was with military intelligence and that he was assigned to the 2-7th Infantry, that he had been at

NTC with Kevin's unit, and had seen Kevin around the company. He said that he could be impartial. He was anything but. He was combative from the start.

According to the regulations for conscientious objection, this was not to be a combative hearing. He asked many questions about Kevin's concerns regarding the competence of his command and did everything he could to push Kevin's buttons. He said that Kevin could not be a conscientious objector because he had not only hunted in the past but that he still owned a hunting rifle. Kevin said that he had not hunted since sometime in the 1990s, but he could not understand how putting food on the table for his family had anything to do with being a conscientious objector to war. The hearing officer argued repeatedly that it was the same. The comment was made that Kevin did not hunt for trophies—we have none. There were times when he did hunt for food. Plenty of people hunt for food simply because they do not have the money to buy the meat. The hearing officer responded by stating if Kevin was truly a conscientious objector, we would just go to the grocery store to buy our meat.

The hearing officer did not want to acknowledge any of my testimony on Kevin's behalf. Even though prior to the start of the hearing and in conversation with Kevin's attorney, he had agreed not to discuss any writing he had found on the Internet in reference to Kevin, he tried several times to bring into question issues raised in the letter I had written in December. This article really bothered all of them, even though none of their names were ever mentioned. He and the members of Kevin's chain of command seemed intent on learning as much as possible about what Kevin knew about his command, based on the one letter I had posted on the Internet alternative media site.

I eventually did admit that I had written the article after a series of questions by the investigating officer, intended as a way to bring the article into the discussion of Kevin's conscientious objector application by my admission rather than his. Kevin's attorney made it clear that this was inappropriate, discussing the action in his rebuttal to the hearing officer's recommendation.

The hearing officer became very agitated. He continued to pressure Kevin, but he could not get Kevin to deviate from his convictions or from discussing his conscientious objector packet. It was clear he was not there to discuss Kevin's position on conscientious objection. It became more and more obvious he was looking for insight into evidence to use against Kevin in Kevin's court-martial, and to learn what Kevin knew about the specific actions of his command. There was never a doubt that this command was going to bring Kevin to court-martial, and were going to use whatever means they had to make it happen. They seemed to be hiding something. At the time we were not clear on what it was. The officer asked leading questions, but Kevin refused to answer any questions that addressed the command.

At the end of the session, the officer was clearly agitated, at one point tossing his pen in the air because he was unable to get the response he wanted from Kevin.

Kevin and his attorney asked for a copy of the officer's handwritten notes from the meeting. The officer responded that he was not required to make them available to them, and denied the request.

Ultimately, after recommending that Kevin's application be denied and receiving Kevin's strong rebuttal to his recommendation, the hearing officer submitted an unheard-of rebuttal of his own in response. It was clear that the command was on the defensive. Kevin's attorney also submitted a demand that the hearing officer produce his copies of the notes he took during the hearing session, along with a list of the questions he posed to Kevin. The attorney won this motion, but strangely, one very important question that had been asked during the hearing, showing the true colors of the command, had been omitted from the list he turned over to Kevin's attorney. The hearing officer stated that the question had not been asked and therefore was deleted, but he had neglected to delete his notes on the answers that Kevin gave to it—one smaller piece of evidence showing the extent this command was willing to go to, to manipulate evidence in prosecuting Kevin for defending the truth.

According to the regulation, the hearing officer was supposed to make his recommendation and submit it to Kevin within two business weeks. He delayed his response as long as he could, then, citing the need to move quickly to avoid violating the deadline imposed by regulations, he insisted that he was not going to allow Kevin the opportunity to submit additional evidence on his behalf. After pressure from Kevin's attorney he finally conceded on this as well. The paperwork for Kevin's conscientious objector application was submitted to the Department of the Army with no time remaining. Five people in the chain of command at Fort Stewart signed form letters saying that they recommended disapproval of the packet. Only one of the five had ever had physical contact with Kevin. None of them had conducted any interviews and no one had been allowed to testify on Kevin's behalf. In the form letter each man initialed, next to "disapproval" was "after careful review." None of these men even knew who Kevin was. They simply signed a form letter, all five of them completing their review in one day. The recommendation was passed up to the Department of the Army. The office in Washington had the hundred-page application packet for sixteen days. It was returned, denied. This had to be one of the shortest considerations ever for a conscientious objector packet. It was clear that no one had reviewed the testimony. No one had any intention of reviewing the testimony. The army simply wanted to close out Kevin's conscientious objector application in time to say it had been denied and could not be used as evidence in his impending court-martial.

Included in the back of the packet that went to the Department of the Army was a memorandum ordered by the lieutenant colonel who commanded Kevin's battalion. This memorandum was prepared by a captain assigned to this detail while in Iraq. The investigative memo had been prepared on January 12, but the lieutenant colonel's directive ordering the investigation was dated January 18. The investigation was to determine if any of the allegations discussed in the letter I had posted on the Internet news site had any validity. The company commander answered all the questions himself. No other witnesses were questioned. The investigation regarding issues of concern at Fort Stewart took place in Iraq. Kevin was not made aware of the investigation. It was interesting that these men felt it necessary to conduct this investigation into their company's actions. Kevin had served with three different commands during the year, and the letter I wrote addressed command performance. I mentioned no one by name in my letter, and yet this command saw a reason to order an investigation and knew specifically what the allegations I had made applied to. They answered the allegations as if they were the ones being accused because they recognized their own actions.

The completed investigation was submitted to the Department of the Army at the back of the packet for Kevin's conscientious objector application. This investigation had nothing to do with Kevin's conscientious objector application and should not have been included. The hearing officer hid the memo in the back of Kevin's packet. He never told Kevin or his attorney that this was part of the evidence he collected.

At no time during the conscientious objector hearing did the hearing officer present to Kevin any of the evidence or witnesses he had gathered. The regulation governing conscientious objection states clearly that an applicant has the right to question any witnesses who provide testimony for his application. Kevin was not granted this right during his hearing. In the final recommendation for the Department of the Army, the hearing officer presented sworn testimony from the staff sergeant who had recommended Kevin to the promotion board and the first sergeant who had given Kevin an excellent NCO evaluation prior to leaving Iraq. In their statements for the conscientious objector application, each asserted that Kevin was a poor soldier who always "railed against the system," thus contradicting their own record and actions prior to Kevin's filing a conscientious objector application. Basically, the two senior NCOs fabricated testimony in their statements, with the testimony reflecting the direction in which the hearing officer wanted their remarks to go.

The staff sergeant stated that all Kevin talked about was hunting and shooting. He recalled conversations with Kevin that had never occurred. Kevin did not trust the man, and he was not given to discussing personal matters with anyone he didn't trust.

The platoon sergeant had always treated Kevin respectfully, giving him as much leadership control as Kevin could have. He sent Kevin out on missions others would not take and relied on Kevin in situations where he knew strong leadership mattered. In his sworn statement to the hearing officer, the platoon sergeant's testimony contradicted his own previously documented statements by saying that he finally had to stop sending Kevin out on missions in Iraq to keep Kevin from questioning the validity of the missions. He mentioned that while in Iraq, someone from the Department of Defense had investigated his unit because of letters that Kevin sent back about the orders the soldiers were given. This investigation occurred while Kevin was still with his unit in Iraq, and no mention of their concern over Kevin's actions was ever made until the testimony for Kevin's conscientious objector application. It just seemed clear to us that the manner in which the command at every level handled Kevin's application was nothing more than a vendetta against a dedicated soldier who told the truth to protect those with whom he served.

4: The Courts-Martial

Monica Kevin and I went back to the company after the conscientious objector hearing so that Kevin could report to his rear detachment commander to be released for the day. After Kevin reported to the captain, the officer told Kevin that he was going to issue Kevin a counseling statement within the next day or so. Kevin asked the captain why, knowing he hadn't done anything that warranted a counseling statement. The captain said that the prosecuting attorneys for Kevin's court-martial had told him that he would have to counsel Kevin and give him a legal order to deploy so that Kevin could refuse to deploy to a superior commissioned officer. This determination was made just two days after the Article 32 hearing in which it was learned that no officer had ever actually given Kevin an order to deploy.

Kevin called his attorney and informed him of what had been said. The attorney went directly to the lead prosecutor to inquire about the prosecution's position. The prosecutor admitted to having told the captain to issue the order in counseling-statement form, saying it had been something that was being considered, but after speaking with the defense attorney, it would not be followed through. The attorney called

Kevin and told him what was said. The attorney was pretty amazed at how unbelievable this was and brought up the question of prosecutorial misconduct. Kevin had already invoked his Article 31 rights to not make statements without representation present and could no longer be legally questioned without his attorney present. The prosecutors did not seem to believe it was necessary to play by the rules.

Two days after the defense attorney had talked to the prosecutors, Kevin was called into his rear detachment commander's office. Even though he was now represented by counsel, which the prosecutors had been reminded of just days before, and even though he had been read his rights five times, one of the prosecutors was sitting in the captain's office, waiting. The captain told Kevin that he had a counseling statement in which he was going to give Kevin an order to deploy. Kevin called me and asked me to try to contact his defense attorney. Kevin finally did reach the attorney, having told the captain he would do nothing without his attorney present.

A short while later Kevin's attorney showed up at the company office with a tape recorder. He taped the prosecution responding to his question of whether the prosecutor remembered the meeting in his own office two days earlier in which he said that the prosecution had considered this but was not going to follow through. The prosecution stated for the record that it had once again changed its mind and ordered the counseling statement anyway. It seemed that the convening authority—the officer who had complete control over the outcome of Kevin's court-martial—exerted influence in every direction he could. Every action was clearly one more measure of the depth of the vendetta being carried out against Kevin for having made a public statement of truth against this command.

February–April, 2005—The Setup

Monica At no point during the conscientious objector hearing did the investigating officer, the military intelligence officer for the 2-7th Infantry (Kevin's unit), ever make it known to Kevin or his attorney that he had witnesses who would testify against Kevin. Kevin should have had an opportunity to address these witnesses; the conscientious objector hearing is not supposed to be a confrontational hearing, and it is not judicial in nature.

To quote Kevin's military attorney in a rebuttal to the recommendation:

> Most damning to Sgt. Benderman, among the litany of errors and issues present, is the fact that Cpt. Aqueche added documents and statements to the file after the hearing. In other words, the IO [investigating officer] added evidence to the record after the hearing and without providing notice to Sgt. Benderman or his counsel. This act by him was arguably unethical and further representative of the biased officer we have had forced upon us. See Para 2-6e, AR 600-43.
>
> First, it appears that Cpt. Aqueche sought statements from several of Sgt. Benderman's former NCO supervisors. MSG [Master Sergeant] Gibbons and SSG [Staff Sergeant] South are two of those NCOs from whom statements were obtained. MSG Gibbons continues at Sgt. Benderman's previous Ft. Hood unit. We question how Cpt. Aqueche could have known of these NCOs except through the criminal law section of OSJA [Office of the Staff Judge Advocate], Ft. Stewart. Indeed, the Defense had previously provided these names to the Government in its Article 32 witness list submitted in February. . . . Then, there is the unexplained presence of a six-page commander's inquiry in the IO's post-hearing file. The document is dated 12 January 2005, although the investigating officer's appointment memo is dated 18 January 2005. The investigation was directed by LTC [Lieutenant Colonel] Todd R. Wood, Sgt. Benderman's former Battalion CO [commanding officer], and was for the apparent purpose of determining whether certain claims Sgt. Benderman allegedly made in a website article were "just or not." LTC Wood also directed the IO, Cpt. Ramon Osorio, to determine whether Sgt. Benderman had violated the UCMJ. It must be pointed out that, until now, Sgt. Benderman was never informed that an investigation pertaining to him had been directed. In addition, he was never questioned nor provided with a copy of the investigative report. Ironically, Cpt. Victor Aqueche, a CO [conscientious objector] hearing investigator who said in his own memo that the CO hearing was not to be an "adverse proceeding," saw it fit to drum up this unrelated and adverse document in an apparent effort to bolster his undeniable intent to pursue a negative recommendation on Sgt. Benderman's CO application. Then, he slipped it into the middle of the morass of copied articles which make up the "record of proceedings." Again, neither Sgt. Benderman nor his counsel received notice of the IO's intent to add these documents.

The IO has also failed to comply with AR 600-43, Para 2-5j, in that he has failed to even authenticate the hearing record.

The two witnesses that the hearing officer interviewed were former supervisors of Kevin's. There is no way the hearing officer could have known who these men were without the help of the prosecutor's office, which was trying to find evidence to use against Kevin in an effort to bolster the very weak case it had filed against him.

The supervisors who were questioned were clearly led in their sworn statements, as evidenced by the staff sergeant's statement completed in the form of distinct questions, all designed to portray Kevin in a negative light.

At the times that Kevin was supervised by these two men, they had both prepared very positive, telling reviews of his performance. The staff sergeant was taking Kevin to the promotion board, and the platoon sergeant participated in the awarding of two Commendation Medals for Kevin's service in Iraq. The platoon sergeant also wrote a highly commendable rating for Kevin's NCO evaluation, dated for the time period that Kevin served in Iraq. It was clear from the comments and from the history that these men were solicited to present damning statements against a soldier they had previously held in very high regard.

March 2005

Monica Kevin continued to work at the duties assigned by his rear detachment supervisors. Life at home continued on as well. We worked in the yard, took the dogs walking on the trails, and we built a chicken coop. Kevin had decided that he wanted fresh eggs, and we had plans for one day living with enough acreage to have a small working farm, so why not start with the chickens now? Leftover building materials were being thrown away at Fort Stewart, so Kevin brought some home and fabricated a coop under the pine trees at the back of the yard. The chickens were a fun diversion. We brought home five Buff Orpington chicks from a local feed store. Just saying their variety name was worth a laugh. We named them, gave them a heat lamp, and watched them grow. They were quite friendly, and with the coop out under the trees, it became a good excuse to get a cup of coffee and sit outside and take a break from the madness the army seemed intent on perpetuating in our lives.

We also had a feral cat that seemed to feel our yard was a safe place to bring her kittens. One day while Kevin and I were checking on the chickens, we saw something small dart through the fence out of the coop and run to the woods. Later, when I went back to see that the chickens were closed up for the night, I saw what had run away earlier. Nestled between the wings of two of the chickens was a tiny gray kitten. That little kitten became the chickens' pet. It slept in the coop nestled under their wings; it ate its kitten chow on the ground near the chicken feeder and drank from the same water bottle. Chickens, kitten, ants, and the rest all served to remind us that it was possible for beings with very different expectations from life to coexist peacefully.

The officers in charge of prosecuting Kevin continued with their mad attempts to make things as difficult as possible, and Kevin was informed that the Article 32 hearing officer had referred his case to court-martial and the convening authority had made it official. The military defense attorney who had taken Kevin's case was the chief trial defense counsel at Fort Stewart. He had detailed himself to Kevin's case from the onset. He was stable, intelligent, and very aware of what was being done by the prosecution, hearing officers, and rear detachment command. He was available and did everything he could to defend Kevin according to the law. People of integrity serve in many different positions within the military. They believe in the soldiers, they have the best interest of the soldiers in mind, and they do what they can in a much disorganized and at times dysfunctional system, to see that the soldiers are treated as human beings. Kevin's military defense attorney was one of those people.

March 19, 2005

Monica We were invited to attend a peace rally in Youngstown, Ohio, for the anniversary of the invasion of Iraq. We had been invited to several different events, but this was a small one with a focus on peace rather than sending an antiwar message. It made perfect sense that this was the event we would attend. It was also at the behest of a very special man and woman. This man had been a conscientious objector during the Korean War and had been an instrumental figure in the antiwar activities during the Vietnam war. His wife had been a draft counselor during Vietnam, and together they were well-respected authorities on the subject of conscientious objection. This man and his wife had been advising us since before Kevin filed his conscientious objector application, and we were honored to have the opportunity to meet them in person.

History is amazing. To have the opportunity to meet those who were such a significant part of the history of this country was equally amazing. When I was a little girl I often sat hidden in the branches of a cherry tree in the yard of my parents' house. I imagined all sorts of adventures. I never imagined the direction my life had now taken. Even with the challenges, it still was not overwhelming; it simply seemed right. There was a part of our life we would eventually reach, but before we got there we had to go through the twists and turns of the road we were now on. I wasn't sure how we would get through it, but I had no doubt that we would. It was important to stay focused on the truth of our experiences—not dramatize it but simply see it all for the reality it was. We needed to think through our actions before we took them, waiting until we were comfortable, knowing that the choice we were making was the right choice, not the easiest one nor one that would compromise the standards we had set for ourselves. It was important to listen to the counsel of others and to respect the lessons they hoped to convey. It was equally important to pay attention and be able to recognize those who sought to influence our actions to suit their personal agenda.

I was grateful for the home we lived in and the quiet life we had made there. We maintained our habits, our routines, and made sure we had private family time. We watched movies together, ate dinner together, worked in the yard, and helped the kids with their needs. Maintaining family values helped anchor our lives, and with that as a priority, it was easier to see when it was time to proceed with caution in dealing with the media, with antiwar organizations, and activist groups.

We encountered many people along the way whose willingness to share their experiences and wisdom was greatly appreciated. I could listen for hours as they spoke of the historic times they had been part of. Something that resonated in the words of all of them was the need to continue the work, and to do so with the same respect for peace that these individuals had demonstrated. Their work was not trivial, and the manner in which we proceeded needed to reflect that. These men and women had acted out of conscience, respecting the choices of others who disagreed, and yet working to try to set an example of peace and a new direction in a way that might lead others to what these peacemakers had already come to know.

Many people in today's "movement" seem to want things to move so quickly. Things were done and then redone when the plan had not been thoroughly investigated and expectations were not met, so it appeared to us that the entire movement was simply spinning in circles. Some people believe it is their responsibility to control how we all arrive at peace; that the peace we all need is somehow their vision rather than the individual peace each of us is entitled to.

It was frustrating. There were times when we felt we were trapped in the middle of two different forms of control—the military, with its skewed sense of discipline, and the peace movement, whose leaders preached human rights but who very much wanted to control the interpretation of those rights. Strangely, both groups professed to be doing the work of peace, and yet they continued to divide the world, putting strains on any hope that a real understanding of peace would be reached. Kevin and I wanted no part of either, to tell the truth. We simply wanted the right to make our own choices and live our lives according to the standards we had set for ourselves. Everyone else was entitled to continue the madness, as long as they left us to our peace.

We cannot bring change when it is not time for change, and justice, more often than not, requires the patience to build a firm foundation. I continued to remind myself of that as we proceeded with Kevin's court-martial. The army clearly wanted things over in a hurry—partly, I'm sure, to keep from having too much media attention on the case. I also believed it felt the quicker the process went along, the less time there was for close scrutiny of the command, and the less likely that anyone would become aware of just how many regulations were not followed and just how little integrity was demonstrated. The command's goal was to punish Kevin to the fullest extent it could. It did not care what regulations it had to manipulate in order to accomplish this objective.

During this time, Kevin and I also met one of the directors of a graduate school in San Francisco who had been developing a Web site devoted to social change. We had many interesting conversations, and in the weeks to come we would work together to create a Web site of our own, which was then linked to this man's Web site for change. He soon became a special friend, and someone whose opinion we valued. This man has a great understanding of the nature of peace and of our goals as far as soldiers' rights and selective conscientious objection. We found our philosophies paralleled each other's in many respects, and the Kevin Benderman Defense Committee Web site (http://www. BendermanDefense.org) became a vehicle not only for informing people of the status of Kevin's case, but also for presenting our philosophy in a way we hoped would generate more public discussions.

March 2005

Monica Toward the end of February Kevin had retained a civilian defense counsel to assist with his court-martial. He had been informed that it would proceed on both charges, Missing Movement and Desertion, and was scheduled to begin on May 10. This attorney and his military counterpart went to the prosecution to discuss the possibility of a plea bargain. The prosecution said no. With Kevin's approval, the civilian counsel made a list of the different options that he might suggest and tried again. The prosecution said no. The lead prosecutor informed the attorneys that the installation commander, also serving as the convening authority with full control over the final decision of the court-martial, had made it clear that he would not accept anything less than Kevin serving the entire length of the deployment in confinement.

During the time that Kevin was waiting for the court-martial to take place, he continued to fulfill his NCO duties. He was at work every day, in uniform, and he did everything his supervisors assigned to him. At one point he was assigned to supervise soldiers returning from AWOL. These soldiers had in most cases been AWOL for four and five months. They had been dropped from the rolls and had missed movement. When they did return it was necessary for them to be processed back into the military so they would once again be listed on the military records. Kevin was one of the NCOs responsible for getting these soldiers processed. Once that was done, these soldiers were then chaptered out of the military, released administratively "for the good of the Army." Kevin was facing court-martial because he filed for conscientious objector status and requested that his application be given the consideration due by regulations and the Constitution. He never missed a day of work and he had a clean record with *no* counseling statements in almost *ten* years. These soldiers, who had been AWOL for over five months and had also missed movement, were chaptered out. One of the soldiers Kevin was assigned to supervise during this time had returned because he was picked up on a DUI charge in Texas. He had been brought back under warrant. He had been AWOL for five months, but he was chaptered out. The picture that evolved from these circumstances was clear. The best thing for a soldier who did not want to deploy was to break the law. If a soldier took the legal means available and pursued an honorable discharge as a conscientious objector, and did so after having already given ten years of honorable service to his country, the soldier would be dealt with in the harshest manner possible. This seemed just a bit hypocritical in light of the fact that enlisted soldiers and officers alike take an oath to defend our Constitution and our laws. Of course, these other soldiers were not publicizing their concerns over the mistreatment they and others were receiving, nor were they calling attention to the lack of organization at the command levels.

A soldier who remained here in Hinesville while he was AWOL had decided that he just didn't want to report for duty. The company commander knew where he was and yet he did nothing to bring him back. After the company deployed, this soldier returned to post. Kevin was assigned to process him back in. Thereafter the soldier sporadically reported to formation for the next two or three weeks, with only a counseling statement issued each time he returned. Several counseling statements were written, and there were many days when he did not show up. Three weeks after he was processed back into the army, the soldier was once again AWOL.

Another picture that developed quite clearly was the fact that Kevin was a quality soldier. He had skills and the highest score possible on the military version of an entrance exam. He was smart and he was mature. The army doesn't care what soldiers of a lesser caliber do, but when a soldier like Kevin publicly speaks out as a conscientious objector, it does not help in the army's propaganda war for new recruits.

It was toward the end of March when we first noticed there was extra pay in Kevin's leave and earnings statement (LES). We didn't do anything about it right away because it is so typical of the army. The Defense Finance and Accounting Service (DFAS) is notorious for making mistakes in a soldier's pay, but it eventually gets around to fixing it.

We had a history of dealing with mistakes by the DFAS. When Kevin was deployed, he did not receive benefits as a married soldier for the duration of the time he was deployed. It didn't matter that much then financially because I was working full-time. When he finally got back to Fort Hood from Iraq, he had to push DFAS to get the back pay. DFAS finally paid, $6,000 of it, but it took almost six months to have the problem rectified.

April 2005

Monica On the April LES, the increase was there again. It had been retroactive to January beginning in March. Kevin called DFAS, but the staff said that he would have to take it up with his command.

Kevin had requested leave on March 30 and had filed an LES with it, as required by regulations. Before he could bring the DFAS problem to the attention of his commanders, they had already noticed it on the LES he included with his leave form. We were scheduled to go to Chicago for weekend speaking events on April 8 and the organizers had already booked flights. The rear detachment commander denied Kevin's leave, and the two staff sergeants serving as rear detachment financial officers for the company told Kevin not to expect any pay in his May LES. They were going to take the back pay out and see that his LES was corrected. We had no choice but to cancel the trip.

Kevin did not do anything more about the situation. We both believed that it had been handled by his rear detachment command.

Kevin received word that his conscientious objector application was being sent to the Department of the Army on April 6. On April 22 it was back in the staff judge advocate's (SJA) office, but Kevin did not receive a copy of it until the following week. It was turned down that quickly. No one could have reviewed it that fast. Kevin immediately turned around and prepared another one. He wrote new essays and gathered new evidence including witness statements and comments and resubmitted it through the chain of command, all the way to the convening authority. A clause in the regulation for conscientious objection allows this. A soldier whose first application for conscientious objection is denied has the right to file a new claim. This new claim must then be processed with the same authority as the initial claim, as long as there is new evidence to support the second application.

It was obvious that the investigating officer was determined to get the conscientious objector application filed as quickly as he did so that the request would be denied before the court-martial convened on the date scheduled in May.

Kevin prepared five copies of the entire second application. He put in a request with the rear detachment commander that he wanted to have a meeting with every member of the chain of command who would have a part in making a personal recommendation on Kevin's application, including the conscientious objector investigating officer. He did not tell them specifically the reason for his request. They arranged for the meeting to be scheduled. At some point the SJA's office caught wind of the request, which threw everything into a tailspin. No one knew why Kevin was calling the meeting, and no one wanted him talking to all of these witnesses right before the court-martial was scheduled to start. Once OSJA canceled the meeting, everyone was basically given leave to go home. For the next two weeks none of these people were available on post. The prosecutors were that concerned about those in the command seeing Kevin or talking to him. Kevin took the conscientious objector application to his military defense attorney, who then submitted the new application for him.

In the two weeks prior to the court-martial, Kevin was told by one of the rear detachment NCOs in charge (NCOIC) that one of the soldiers in his squad, another sergeant, remembered the command sergeant major coming out of his office after Kevin had left the scheduled meeting with him on January 7 and telling the sergeant that he had released Kevin. Apparently this soldier had been the sergeant assigned to the duty desk that night. It was difficult for the defense to locate the sergeant for questioning as he had been reassigned to a medical hold unit. Kevin's attorneys listed both the NCOIC and the sergeant as witnesses for the defense. In time, the sergeant did speak with the defense attorney and confirmed what the NCOIC had reported to Kevin. The defense attorney had the distinct impression that the sergeant did not want to be involved. He wanted to make sure that his discharge was not affected by his testifying as a witness for the defense. One day after the attorneys had met with the sergeant, Kevin was leaving the company when he noticed the sergeant leaving Kevin's rear detachment commander's office. This was strange, because the sergeant had been reassigned to the medical hold unit several weeks ago, which meant there was no longer any reason for him to have any communication with the captain of Kevin's rear detachment unit.

Another sergeant was available who was assigned as the duty sergeant to replace the soldier who was on duty when the sergeant major reported Kevin released after their meeting. He was willing to testify that no one gave anyone an order to call Kevin nor did anyone give an order for any soldier to drive by our house to locate Kevin, nor was the military police called to bring Kevin into custody and make him deploy with his unit.

May 2005—The First Court-Martial

Monica The first court-martial was scheduled for May 11. The motions were to be argued on May 10. The defense filed a motion to suppress statements submitted by the command sergeant major regarding the meeting on January 7 and by the rear detachment commander on January 18. (They claimed these statements were made by Kevin. The defense said that they were taken illegally.)

On every occasion available to him, the rear detachment commander made comments about Kevin being handcuffed and in leg-irons once he was convicted. This captain seemed fairly confident of a conviction. He spoke with Kevin's supervisor and another NCOIC who was close to Kevin and assigned them to escort Kevin from the courtroom. He made them go to central supply on post and sign out a set of leg-irons and handcuffs. Neither one of these soldiers felt comfortable being in this position.

Kevin's defense attorneys filed a motion for a new Article 32 hearing because of an implication of bias demonstrated by the actions of the investigating officer assigned to Kevin's case. In a series of e-mail exchanges between the investigating officer, the SJA, and the convening authority, none of which were forwarded to Kevin's defense attorneys, the investigating officer made a comment across the top of one page alluding to her belief that Kevin had not deserted during Operation Iraqi Freedom I, which was when she shared a working relationship with Kevin's military defense attorney. The implication was that she believed that he did desert during the deployment to Operation Iraqi Freedom III. The e-mail exchanges were a direct result of the defense attorney's request to the judge advocate to not appoint this particular lieutenant colonel as investigating officer in Kevin's case. The comments by the lieutenant colonel were made in an effort to justify her right to the appointment. The defense attorneys called this to the judge's attention in a motion to dismiss the case because of the investigating officer's indiscretion.

The government (as the army was represented during the court-martial) filed a pretrial motion in limine brief asking to prevent the defense from using Kevin's conscientious objector application, his change of beliefs, and his eyewitness experiences in Iraq as part of his defense. The government, however, would still be able to use the conscientious objector application against Kevin. There were several items of interest in the motion filed by the government. It insisted that Kevin had reenlisted for another tour of duty after he had returned from Iraq in 2003. It was the army's assertion that Kevin could not be sincere in his application for conscientious objection if he was willing to reenlist after serving a combat tour in Iraq. A major discrepancy in this line of reasoning was the clear, proven fact that Kevin had reenlisted in 2002, almost five months prior to the invasion of Iraq. A second inconsistency was the government's argument that Kevin had traveled throughout the country "railing against government policy and the actions of the administration in regard to Iraq," and therefore his intent to refuse deployment was clearly political and he could not be sincere in his application for conscientious objection. This was another major fallacy. There was no evidence of any aspect of these statements. Kevin and I had, in fact, traveled to two cities in the course of the time leading up to his court-martial. In both instances, the events centered on conscientious objection and the justification for a soldier's right to expect consideration of changing beliefs regarding war.

The government's motion was never argued before the judge. Kevin's court-martial was dismissed before it had even started. The judge found in favor of the defense's motion to dismiss on the grounds that the investigating officer had demonstrated implied bias in her actions prior to the Article 32 hearing.

That evening, May 10, at the completion of the court-martial proceedings, we were sitting in our attorney's office when the prosecution attorneys called the defense attorneys to a meeting in their office. When the attorneys returned, they told Kevin that the prosecution was talking about bringing larceny charges against him. At that point, we had no idea why. The civilian attorney suggested to Kevin that it would be in Kevin's best interests to just plead guilty to missing movement, take what he thought would be twelve to eighteen months, and be done. Kevin immediately said no. He had done nothing wrong. Kevin's attorneys also said that the chief prosecutor was pressing to bring the larceny charges, but that the lead prosecutor was against it. The lead prosecutor stated that he only had one vote, however, and couldn't stop the others if they decided to go ahead with the charges. The chief prosecutor said that if Kevin reverted to the original Article 32 investigation findings and allowed a new court-martial to proceed using those findings, he would not file the larceny charges. But Kevin was not going to do that so the chief prosecutor brought new charges against Kevin for larceny in addition to missing movement and desertion. There was no evidence to convict Kevin for missing movement. He had been released by his command sergeant major and nothing existed that could refute that important fact. In order for the command to proceed to a new court-martial after the judge dismissed the first court-martial in the manner he had, the prosecution was going to have to bring new charges to justify a new Article 32 hearing.

Interestingly, the lieutenant colonel who had served as the SJA until this point recused himself from the case.

May 11 was the date that the new Article 32 hearing started, since the initial court-martial had been dismissed. New testimony was presented from the chain of command, which was then stationed in Iraq but had returned for the court-martial. The sergeant on duty the night Kevin attended the meeting with his sergeant major also testified. He said that he was on duty the night of the meeting. He was shown a duty log and asked if he recognized it. He said that there were some entries on it that were in his writing, but there were several that were made during the times that he was on duty that were not in his writing. The duty log showed an entry at 1710 hours stating that the sergeant major had said that Kevin had refused to deploy, but this entry was not made in the duty sergeant's handwriting. The statement that I had witnessed during the meeting with the sergeant major clearly refuted that particular entry. I had noted the time of my witness to the statement as 1738 on the form. With the exception of Kevin leaving briefly to go to the copy machine and make a copy of the statement that I signed, no one left the meeting room until 1800 hours.

When it came time for the second court-martial in July, the staff duty sergeant was placed on the witness list for the defense. Unfortunately the sergeant was nowhere to be found. He had been discharged and was somewhere in Oklahoma, and the prosecution informed the newly appointed judge that it would take some time to locate an address for him, a matter that would delay the proceedings. The judge, in the interest of saving time, ordered the defense to stipulate to the testimony of this particular witness. This meant that there would be no testimony from him. He could not be found. The NCOIC who had reported hearing details of the conversation between this sergeant and the sergeant major on the night of the meeting did testify regarding the sergeant's statement, but without the sergeant himself to testify, it was only hearsay.

The command that needed to return to Iraq was questioned by the new investigating officer, a commander who had returned from Iraq in March. The rest of the Article 32 hearing was to reconvene at the end of June regarding the larceny charges and also with any further testimony from other witnesses.

The day after this fiasco, May 12, I received a phone call. The voice sounded distinctly like Kevin's company commander. When I said, "Hello," his response was, "Tell your husband, I am going to see that he goes to prison—coward!" And then he hung up.

Two days later, Kevin received word that his second conscientious objector application was not going to be processed. Clearly the command and convening authority were not going to show any respect to Kevin's rights according to the UCMJ.

May 2005

Monica Even when things were incredibly difficult, I found it best to remain focused on us and know that for everything negative, there is also a positive. In the situation we were now facing, the facts were clear: Kevin had done nothing wrong. He had followed army regulations. He had followed the law. He had kept his word and not backed down from the principles he had chosen to live by. Everything we had done in this situation had been done honestly, and there was nothing to be ashamed of in our actions. Not everyone would necessarily agree with the choice Kevin made, but that is the beauty of life. We, as human beings, do not all have to agree with how we choose to live. We only must agree on allowing each other the right to decide for ourselves what that choice will be.

We remained in contact with soldiers that Kevin had served with. We heard from many other members of the military, active duty and retired. It was never Kevin's or my intention to disrespect the beliefs of any of the men and women who had served this country in the military. We had experienced firsthand what so many others had also been through. We understood the separation, the training, the commitment, and the sacrifice that were all part of military service. We understood the detachment from emotions that was necessary for survival, and the struggle to come to terms with those emotions when they began to surface as conscience took over and the mind could no longer shut down the memory of the experiences we had faced. Kevin's application for conscientious objection and my support of his decision were individual choices. Every aspect was carefully considered, including the effect his decision would have on the soldiers he served with and their family members. Outside of our own family, they were the ones that mattered most. Kevin was making a personal choice to no longer participate in war at a time when thousands of soldiers would be facing repeated deployments to a very difficult war zone.

While we made the decisions that were best for us, we wanted to be certain that our choice did not detract from the message we wanted to convey. Military personnel and their families need support. Not the kind of support that shows itself in yellow ribbons and flag waving. Not the support that is another's opinion of whether a decision made is right or wrong. The support needed by those men and women willing to put their lives on the line to keep Americans safe is when Americans give equally in their commitment to keeping the soldiers safe in return.

I appreciated the support we received from activists of all kinds from all over the world. So many people, old, young, children, all wrote to offer kind words and thoughts on their feelings of war and peace. It gave me a sense of just how small our great big world can be.

What was troubling, however, was the ease with which so many of the peace-loving activists were willing to condemn our soldiers unless they chose to walk the path of resistance and take steps on the road these activists had declared was the only right way to go. They spoke of our being heroes, Kevin for the actions he took and me for supporting him. They wanted to hold us up as special for having made a personal choice to live by our own standards and not allow the choices of others to dictate our actions. They criticized soldiers who continued to serve for not having made the same decision Kevin had. I didn't feel very heroic, and I don't think Kevin did either.

As we progressed through the courts-martial process, I appreciated the work of those who hoped to move us closer to peace, and yet I appreciated the dedication of the soldiers and their families even more. Their commitment was one that only those in the military could understand. The pain and the sacrifice that accompanied their dedication were felt with an emotion that defied a simple verbal description—especially to people who did not seem to want to understand. The only way they would come to appreciate it was to live through it themselves, and to survive.

The lack of trust I felt for civilians during the time my husband was at war came back to haunt me when Kevin and I were faced with his impending courts-martial. We received letters and cards from all over the world. People in thirty-nine different countries applauded the sacrifice we had made in defense of peace. We chose to make the decision for Kevin to file for conscientious objector status, trusting that the citizens of this country would hold the commanders accountable to the regulations that gave Kevin the legal right to choose as he did. We based this on the words they spoke to us.

When Kevin's case became public, we spoke with everyone we could about the need to support the soldiers. The reason the command chose to punish Kevin so harshly was simply because he spoke the truth about conditions the soldiers faced, just as we spoke together about the lack of support both soldiers and their families received for the sacrifices they made. People gave lip-service responses. We heard activists proclaim themselves to be *for* the cause of the soldiers. Leaders in antiwar organizations and veterans' groups wrote, expressing their support and willingness to do what they could to help bring about changes to what the soldiers were forced to deal with. We listened to their words and counted on them to follow through with their promises. We had hoped that they would be there as they said they would.

Many other soldiers watched how Kevin's case was handled by the military and by those in the peace movement. In the end, it was clear that few people keep their word to soldiers, except those who have walked in their boots. The brotherhood that exists among those who have served is a strong and powerful connection. I came to understand it well. For those who have been through the very real fire of fighting to survive, when it is life on the edge, only those who have also put their lives into the fire and survived will understand with any feeling just what it means to have served. Those who gave more than words to our actions are those we came to care about, because they understood survival, having faced the need in their own lives.

Just a few weeks before the first court-martial we received a phone call from a man who became family to us. We had been scheduled to attend some events in Chicago during the month of April, to speak about Kevin's position regarding conscientious objection when the rear detachment commander decided not to approve Kevin's leave request and the trip was canceled. Shortly thereafter, a Franciscan priest called to introduce himself to us, and as we spoke, it seemed that we had known him for a very long time. He had planned on meeting with us in Chicago and was disappointed the meeting didn't happen. He wondered if we would mind if he attended Kevin's upcoming court-martial. Without hesitation we asked him to stay with us during his visit. This man has given so much of himself to the cause of peace, and he has incredible peace in his heart. We spent the evenings during the week leading up to the court-martial sitting and listening to him talk about his experiences. His manner is quiet and humble. He is giving, and his presence added to the sense of calm both Kevin and I already felt during this time. We were faced with challenges, but there was a way through, and we would find it by moving forward, the only direction we planned on taking.

June 2005 — New Investigations

Monica The new Article 32 hearing reconvened on June 26. This hearing was entirely about the larceny charges, with the exception of some additional questions for the rear detachment commander regarding the first two charges filed.

Based on the questions asked by the new investigating officer, we felt confident that the larceny charges would ultimately be dismissed. When the hearing officer's recommendation was returned, he strongly recommended that the larceny charges be dropped as they were obviously the result of an accounting error on the part of the command. A soldier could not have been the cause of receiving extra money in a paycheck from the army. It was also obvious that none of the other eighty-five soldiers at Fort Stewart who had also received the extra money were being given any judicial discipline for the error. Kevin was the only soldier to be charged with larceny for an accounting oversight, and the prosecutor testified during the Article 32 hearing that he was charging Kevin with larceny but not the other soldiers, because none of the other soldiers was being court-martialed. Since Kevin was already being brought up on other charges, that set him apart from the other soldiers, and therefore the larceny charges were valid. When questioned by the defense during the court-martial, the prosecutor stated that he believed it was Kevin's intent to steal the money from the government based on the fact that Kevin had hired a civilian attorney and obviously would need the money to pay for his representation. The prosecutor knew that a soldier made very little in the way of salary, and therefore Kevin's circumstances led the prosecutor to believe that he would steal the money to settle his financial situation.

July 2005—The Second Court-Martial

Monica The new investigating officer submitted his recommendations following the completion of the second Article 32 hearing. In addition to recommending dismissal of the larceny charges, he also expressed his concern over the validity of the remaining two charges, missing movement by design, and desertion, although he felt there was some evidence that warranted the court-martial to move forward. The convening authority pressed forward on all charges in spite of the recommendations of the investigating officer, and the court-martial was scheduled to begin pretrial motions on July 20.

We had no expectations regarding the outcome of Kevin's trial. This was the army, and the command running things at Fort Stewart didn't seem to care much for the regulations, at least not when it came to Kevin's trial. Regardless of the outcome, at some point it would all be over. Life moved on. We worked on our Web site, talked with many members of the media, and pursued a discussion of conscientious objection with as many people as would join us. Word of Kevin's case traveled across the world and did so very quickly. We were invited to interviews on radio programs, for newspapers, and on television in countries all over the world, including Australia, Great Britain, Japan, Canada, Germany, Greece, France, Italy, Poland, Jordan—even Iran. Many people wanted to hear our opinions on the Iraq war and the administration's foreign policy.

We spoke of conscientious objection. We would maintain our personal beliefs regarding the war and foreign policy, but our beliefs were based on the information we had gathered, our personal education.

People were listening to what we had to say, and it seemed that many of those people were very easily influenced. It would have been inappropriate for us to address issues publicly when we did not have all the facts. So much of what was being done at this time regarding the direction of our country appeared to come from misrepresentations, misinterpretations, and misunderstandings. What we knew was based on our firsthand experiences. What we could speak of with clarity and honesty were those firsthand experiences, and an explanation of our actions as a result of those experiences. People were going to have to decide for themselves what to believe with regard to the Iraq war and foreign policy by educating themselves as we had.

We received so many cards and letters from children. The most beautiful hand-drawn pictures and cards came to us from the Netherlands, Canada, New York, and Washington. We were asked to allow statements we had made regarding conscientious objection to be included in a textbook for students in Brazil. Children as young as five wrote descriptions of their own vision for peace. There was no way we could respond to every child, to every person who wrote. We hoped that our continued actions would serve to show them that we cared what they thought; we knew they were watching. We wanted to be sure of every decision we made—to know it was the right one for us, not the one we felt others would want us to make. We wanted people to know that peace comes from all of us living in the best way possible for ourselves and our families.

July 28, 2005

Monica Two motions filed by the defense would be considered prior to the actual start of the court-martial. The week before, in consideration of a pretrial motion by the defense, the judge dismissed the larceny charges, as we had hoped. We knew they were being used for intimidation more than anything else. The larceny charges were one more attempt by this command to use whatever means possible to threaten Kevin and bring him back under control. What his commanders didn't seem to realize was that Kevin had done nothing wrong; therefore, threats would not work.

The judge heard arguments for suppressing statements the prosecution wanted to use in testimony against Kevin. Kevin had invoked his rights several times during the course of the command's investigation into charges against him. The command continually disregarded this in its own administrative questioning leading to its decision to file charges against Kevin. The basis for the case against Kevin was a statement written by the command sergeant major in which he claimed that Kevin refused a direct order to deploy during a meeting held the night of their company's deployment.

Two Iraq war veterans, both declared conscientious objectors, had driven here to be with us for Kevin's court-martial. We appreciated their support. They understood more than others, for they had already faced what we were now in the middle of. It was good to meet them and to hear them recount their own experiences with the military. We spent the evening before the court-martial reliving experiences, sharing perspectives, and getting acquainted with new friends.

The morning of the twenty-eighth arrived as any other. Kevin was awake before light and soon had coffee perking. It wasn't long before it was time to drive on post and meet with the attorneys before walking to the courtroom.

Exactly one week earlier there had been another court-martial at Fort Stewart. This one involved a soldier who had gone AWOL to avoid deployment and later returned to file a conscientious objector application. While his application was being considered, he again went AWOL on the day his unit deployed. He was subsequently picked up in another state on a warrant issued by the military and held in pretrial custody. The cast of characters was surprisingly familiar. He shared Kevin's defense attorneys, both civilian and military, and the prosecutors were the same, as was the judge hearing the case.

We were in the trial defense attorney's office when his verdict was returned. Despite having been AWOL, deserting his unit twice to avoid deployment, and having been returned on a warrant, this soldier received only six months' confinement. The defense attorneys were pleased with the result and felt it boded well for justice in Kevin's case. Kevin had not broken any regulations. With the judge demonstrating fairness in this soldier's case, there was reason to believe she would display the same clarity and fairness in Kevin's case.

I didn't have a premonition about the outcome of Kevin's court-martial. There would be issues to deal with no matter what decision was made, unless the judge was allowed to hear evidence regarding the manner in which the command mishandled Kevin's conscientious objector application. If that evidence could be presented, it would be easy to see that the command sought to punish Kevin for speaking the truth about its faulty leadership. If the evidence regarding the lack of support in handling the soldiers' concerns with this command were put in front of the judge, including the unjust treatment of Kevin's right to conscientious objection, there would be reason to believe that someone in the military justice system actually had enough integrity to see that justice was served. The command, the prosecution, and those advising both were doing everything they could to prevent Kevin from using his beliefs, firsthand experiences, and his application for conscientious objection in his defense. We wondered what they were afraid of. If they believed what they were saying to be the truth, then they should not have been concerned about any evidence Kevin presented in his defense. The truth can be quite scary, and the command was clearly worried.

The court-martial was over almost before it began. The defense motion to include the only evidence of significance regarding the meeting in which Kevin was released by the sergeant major was suppressed. The sergeant major admitted to having written the statement after Kevin had invoked his rights, and in reference to a hypothetical question and response in the context of a conversation in which his rank had no authority, thereby making the statement inadmissible.

I was the only witness to testify on Kevin's behalf. The events of the meeting with the sergeant major were the defining events, and Kevin, the sergeant major, and I were the only individuals who participated. There was clearly no evidence to convict Kevin. The sergeant major gave conflicting testimony to his own testimony. His statements clearly showed him to be an unreliable witness, and there were no other witnesses to the meeting. Other members of the chain of command testified for the prosecution, but their testimony could only be defined as hearsay. The rear detachment commander who had brought the charges against Kevin had not even been in the state at the time the meeting with the sergeant major took place. By all accounts, the decision of the judge should have been to declare Kevin innocent of all charges. At several points during the testimony put forth by prosecution witnesses, the judge could be seen shaking her head in apparent disbelief. Her body language showed that she was unsure why this case had even been brought to court-martial.

In closing arguments Kevin's civilian defense attorney spelled it out clearly. The most the judge could find was that this was a case of a three-day AWOL.

In his own closing arguments, the lead prosecutor directed the judge to find Kevin guilty on both charges, and give him the maximum punishment allowable to send a clear message to other soldiers that they should not consider using conscientious objection as a way to get out of going to war.

Even the prosecution witnesses appeared nervous that Kevin was about to be released and the case dismissed. In truth, there was no other decision for the judge to make.

When she returned to the courtroom after deliberation, her first action was to dismiss the desertion charge. This brought a sigh of relief. She then returned a verdict of guilty for missing movement and sentenced Kevin to fifteen months in confinement, and the room fell silent. No one had believed such an outcome possible, based on the testimony and lack of evidence. It was clear that something had happened in the back room that no one else was privy to. Justice was not served in the courtroom on Fort Stewart this day.

Kevin turned around to look at me. We were startled, angry, dumbfounded, and shocked. He came to the bar between us and put his arms around me—it was what I needed. I saw him looking back through the courtroom to where those in the chain of command sat watching. The decision had been made. Whatever we now had to face, we would face. There was a reason, and there was also a solution. Something was not right with this decision—not just that there had been no evidence presented that warranted this decision, but also that Kevin and I knew it was based on a clear misrepresentation of facts. Kevin and I knew, without doubt, that he had not refused an order to deploy. We knew he had been released after the meeting with the sergeant major, and his actions had demonstrated his clear belief in the intent of the sergeant major's order to Kevin that he complete his conscientious objector packet and prepare for the difficult task of proving his sincerity. We would move forward. The next fifteen months would be challenging and lonely, but we would get through them.

After a short time together in the witness room, talking about plans for what was coming, working through what had just happened, and simply being close for a while, we heard people outside the door. There was the sound of chains, which only angered me. The attorneys came in for a few quick instructions and with the appeal paperwork to sign, and it was time for Kevin to leave. The soldier who had been Kevin's supervisor in rear detachment was one of his escorts. I found out later that he made it clear he would not be placing chains on Kevin, there was no need, and Kevin walked out of the courthouse without them. Standing on the steps of the courthouse watching Kevin walk toward the waiting van that would take him to the county jail to serve time until he could be processed for moving to a military prison, I felt an anger I didn't know I could feel. He held his head high, turned around quickly, and I knew how strong Kevin was. I knew how strong I was going to have to be, for the months to come were not going to be easy, and I was going to have to find a way to defend him against what had happened. The army had not made things easy to this point; there was no reason to believe it was going to change now.

After Kevin had been taken to the county jail, his supervisor came and returned his personal belongings. Anger again. I knew I would be given Kevin's wallet, ID cards, and clothes. I did not expect to be given his wedding ring. A cold feeling went through me when the staff sergeant said that the county jail would not let him wear the ring. I called the commander of the county jail to learn when visiting hours would be. He was very helpful and aware of Kevin's case. The people we dealt with at the county jail were understanding and went out of their way to help. It did not stop the anger, but it helped me focus on what I needed to do next.

The Iraq veterans who had come for the court-martial remained for a couple more days. It was good to have them here. They helped me focus as well. As difficult as this time has been, we are fortunate to have met good people along the way who understand the circumstances for having faced their own challenges with the military. One such person was a retired lieutenant colonel from the Vietnam era.

We had somehow connected with him while Kevin was working on his conscientious objector application. He had a radio program with a large following and had taken us under his wing. He had been through his own transformation toward peace and shared his perspective to help us evaluate our own personal journey.

He is a good man. When he heard that Kevin would be facing court-martial, he offered to pay his own way to attend and testify to Kevin's sincerity and character. This meant so much to us. He was contacted by Kevin's civilian attorney, arrangements were made, and we asked him to stay with us while he was here. Kevin had planned to meet him at the airport in Savannah after the initial phase of the court-martial and drive him back to Hinesville to participate in the sentencing phase if necessary. Unfortunately, the court-martial was over and Kevin had been taken to jail before the man's plane had even landed. One of the veterans staying with us went to the airport in Kevin's place.

This man was so generous and helpful during the time that followed. He stayed for several days and gave me a great deal of support. He went with our son and me to visit Kevin at the county jail over the weekend. Kevin had developed tremendous respect for this man over the months we had talked and worked with him. Kevin was disappointed at not being able to meet him at the airport. When the colonel walked into the visiting room, Kevin stood on the other side of the wall and saluted him. It meant a lot to know this man was willing to give that much of himself to be there for us.

It was a strange feeling walking into a jail to visit Kevin. New construction was going on at the jail, and when we arrived we immediately got turned around walking through a maze of unfinished hallways lined with cells, guard centers, and activity rooms. It was dark and I had an unsettling feeling of being lost. It was an appropriate feeling for the next few weeks as Kevin and I became accustomed to the strange circumstances we would now deal with for more than a year to come. We finally arrived at the guard center where we would visit Kevin. After checking in and having them inspect the few items we had brought that Kevin said he needed, we were allowed into the visiting room. The room was off to the side of the guard center, and those on duty could watch the visit from where they sat. When Kevin came in, he was wearing the typical black-and-white striped prison uniform. He was Kevin—he even looked imposing dressed in a prison uniform.

We talked about everything we could think of that hadn't been talked about in the weeks leading up to the court-martial. According to prison regulations, we were only supposed to have one hour of the two-hour visitation time for our visit. The guard commander had already expressed his sympathies over what had happened, and the time limit was overlooked so that we were able to talk for the entire visitation instead.

It was good to have the time. It was reassuring to see that Kevin was OK, that he was strong, and it was good to be able to show him that we would get through the new wave of madness together. I wanted to make sure he knew that no matter what, I did "have his back" and I wouldn't stop working to find someone who was willing to help bring justice to his case. Many people had given their words of support to us over those first eight months, people we would never meet. We knew we could count on each other; as for the rest, we would just have to wait and see.

Life, to me, had come to be like a giant jigsaw puzzle. No two pieces were exactly the same shape, and yet each unique cutout had a way of fitting with those that encircled it so that, once joined, a beautiful picture was created. There are aspects of each piece that belong to the whole: colors, designs, and the final concept. Still, every piece maintains its uniqueness separate from the others.

Human beings are like puzzle pieces to me. There is a reason for each person's uniqueness. We need what only that person can offer in order to complete the final painting we envision for the world to be at peace. When we stop believing we have a right to control what another person becomes and simply live as we are meant to, allowing others to find their place as well, I believe we will be at a place where peace will happen. We are human beings and our basic needs and inherent rights are the same; beyond that, we are vastly different, and our humanity should be celebrated as such.

5: Incarceration

Monica At the time Kevin was sentenced, no one could tell us exactly where he would serve his time. The military attorney thought he would be sent to the prison at Fort Knox, Kentucky, because of the length of his sentence. Over the weekend the staff sergeant who had been Kevin's supervisor and had now become one of the escorts to take him to whatever prison he would end up in, came to the house to help collect all of Kevin's gear. He had also been told that Kevin would probably be sent to Fort Knox but had been given nothing definite.

On Sunday he called and said the command had still not given him anything specific, but that he was to be ready to fly when called and it would be with very little notice. Kevin had liberal use of the phones at the county jail and we talked quite often during the five days he was there. He had heard nothing, and the guards there were kept in the dark as well. None of the secrecy made much sense to me, but after the way everything else had been handled I was not surprised.

I was awakened by a phone call at 3 a.m. on August 1. It was Kevin. The staff sergeant escorting him had allowed him to use his cell phone to call and let me know they were taking him from the county jail to the airport. I was grateful for the staff sergeant. If it hadn't been for him I would not have known that Kevin had even left. Kevin also let me know that he would be serving his time three thousand miles away at Fort Lewis, Washington. This was the farthest possible location from where we lived, and it was obvious that the command had done what it could to make things as difficult as possible for us from beginning to end. What Kevin's commanders didn't know was how little effect they would ultimately have on our relationship, or how ridiculous it had been for them to think they could do anything to keep us from talking about what they had done, or why. They thought they could intimidate us enough that we would simply stop talking and quietly go away. They gave us strength—and we hoped to be able to use our experiences to help educate the civilian world as to just how much support those in the military needed to hold the command structure accountable to the regulations and the humanity of the soldiers and their families.

Kevin The powers that be at Fort Stewart thought they were going to come between Monica and me by sending me to Fort Lewis, Washington, which is about as far away as you can get in the continental United States. What those morons did not realize, evidently, was that what we have together cannot be separated by miles or by the actions of small-minded and immature individuals such as themselves.

Monica The staff sergeant allowed Kevin to use his cell phone at several points along the way from the county jail to Fort Lewis. I appreciated his consideration and knew that Kevin would be treated well with him along. When he returned from Fort Lewis, the staff sergeant came to tell me the specifics of the trip—how Kevin was taken care of and what the facility at Fort Lewis was like. He said that it was really nothing more than a long deployment, and if we looked at it that way we would be able to get through the time more quickly. I went to sleep that night thinking about his words. I realized how true they were, more than I imagine even he knew. I was reminded of when Kevin left Fort Hood to go to Iraq. I compared that experience to what we had just gone through with Kevin leaving for a year in the military prison at Fort Lewis. In the time since Kevin and I were married we had lived through two long deployments. Each time he was sent to war—each experience was meant to achieve peace but with vastly different methods. I felt at peace with both, and I was coming to understand—peace is not something we use our outward experiences to reach for; peace is something we find within ourselves, and it is the strength that allows us to face the challenges of our outward experiences without losing sight of who we are in the process.

Kevin My immediate supervisor was very helpful because he knew what the commanders had done, as they were hostile to the soldiers who did not want to be in their clique and kiss up to them. This group of people was the most power-hungry and clannish I have ever run across in my time in the army. They acted like junior high-schoolers with something to prove to themselves. It is really kind of pathetic that grown men who are in the army command still act like teenagers who are unsure of themselves.

Monica I would have liked to believe the command at Fort Stewart had a bit of humanity within. Its actions proved differently. The rear detachment command was to have called to notify me of Kevin's situation along with the date of his transfer and his final destination. After the sentence was read in the courtroom, the command filed out to stand on the steps of a nearby building and watch Kevin being led away. I saw every member of the chain of command who had banded together to re-create facts, fabricate evidence, and manipulate their stories stand together again and watch Kevin walk away with his head held high. They wanted to gloat—to shout and cheer that they had won. They could not. Even banded together those men were not half as strong as Kevin was walking alone. I did not expect to hear from them after Kevin left. If they had been men of integrity, they would not have been afraid to face me. If they had been men of integrity, there would have been no shame in their actions, and Kevin never would have gone to prison.

Kevin called to let me know that he was safely in Seattle and getting ready for the ride to Fort Lewis, about thirty minutes south of the airport. He called just before they entered the gate at Fort Lewis to let me know he would contact me when he could. Kevin's supervisor was a man of integrity, and I appreciate everything he did to help us during the court-martial, the transfer to Fort Lewis, and during Kevin's time away.

According to regulations, the commander of the Regional Corrections Facility (RCF) at Fort Lewis was to contact me within two weeks of Kevin's arrival to give me information about visiting, about regulations we were required to follow, and to acknowledge that Kevin had arrived there and was being treated with respect. I heard nothing. Two months after Kevin had been taken to Fort Lewis I finally received a letter. It came to me postmarked almost two weeks earlier than it was received. It was not sent until after I had called two congressional representatives, written an article posted on several alternative media Web sites, and e-mailed copies of the article to members of the command at the Fort Lewis RCF.

Kevin The people in charge of the RCF were not following army regulations in any way; they were supposed to send Monica a letter telling her where I was and how to contact me and give her other instructions regarding visitation. They were not going to do what they are required by law to do. So Monica had to get several members of congressional offices involved to force these people to do what they should have been doing as a matter of course.

Monica Kevin and I spoke about the need to remain public. We had heard from so many people inquiring about Kevin and the conditions he faced. We thought about things and decided the best approach would be for Kevin to write a statement that could be posted on our Web site as a way of reassuring people that he was OK and would remain strong even in confinement. His first letter received such a tremendous response that we felt it was important to continue with weekly statements. We managed to find a way for him to communicate his statements to me without having to send each one through the mail. We were reasonably certain that any statements he chose to send by mail would be read, possibly censured, and in some instances simply thrown away. We knew of several inmates at the RCF who had tried to send letters to various public figures over the course of their confinement that had not been mailed. We had little doubt that the RCF staff would welcome the opportunity to silence Kevin.

August–October 2005

Monica After Kevin's sentence was read and we were together in the witness room, the defense attorneys came in with paperwork to ensure that Kevin would be able to file a legal appeal against the judge's decision.

In a military court-martial the judge's decision is not final. The convening authority for the court-martial, generally the commanding officer of the installation where the trial is held, has the final say over the sentence. After the judge renders a decision, a period of ninety days ensues during which time a verbatim record of the trial is prepared, and all court documents are added to the record. The defendant is then allowed to prepare a statement requesting clemency and make any other requests for consideration regarding the case to be included in the final record of the trial. Prosecutors and defense attorneys are able to add their recommendations to the file, and any others who might offer character testimony on behalf of the defendant may also submit brief statements.

The convening authority then considers the entire record of the trial in addition to any documents submitted as recommendations after the judge issued a decision. The convening authority has the power to determine the final sentence either by letting it stand as the judge ordered, or reducing it as it sees fit. The convening authority does not have the authority to make the sentence any harsher. Once the convening authority makes its decision, it is possible for the appeal process to start. The convening authority, in Kevin's case, finalized Kevin's conviction during Kevin's incarceration at Fort Lewis. Kevin's conviction was left to stand as ordered. We had expected nothing less. It was in keeping with the disregard for truth manifested by the chain of command at Fort Stewart from the start as far as Kevin's case was concerned. We hoped for the best, and knew it would not come from this particular group of officers. Once the decision was made, it simply meant that it was time for us to regroup and begin the process of working on Kevin's appeal.

Many hundreds of good people across the country and the world sent letters to the convening authority, the secretary of the army, even the secretary of defense on Kevin's behalf. Most were kind enough to forward copies of their letters to a post office box we had established for people to send letters of support to us during this time. We were amazed at how far-reaching word of Kevin's situation had become. We appreciated everyone's desire to help. The letters made a difference to us, but they didn't affect the decision of the convening authority.

In retrospect, the letters served notice to the military command that Kevin's case was being scrutinized by the public. It did little to lessen the time he had to serve; in fact, it caused the command to be as harsh as the situation would allow in terms of its treatment and discipline of Kevin, at times making it more difficult than most will ever know. Several times over the months Kevin was in prison we considered our choices and had to make a decision whether it was best to continue with the public attention or to simply take a breath, get through the rest of the time as quietly as possible, and let the actions of the command against Kevin simmer down. We could never stop for long, and the discipline continued. Kevin was strong and faced it all head-on. He would do everything he could to see that I received word of what was happening, and I made sure that others knew as well.

Kevin called about three weeks after he had arrived at Fort Lewis. He was concerned that the command there, including the civilian warden, was going to make things as difficult for him as they could. He had asked to meet with the prison chaplain to discuss the situation with his conscientious objector application and to ask the chaplain to help him with an appeal of the army's decision to deny his claim.

Kevin I was starting to get the lay of the land, so to speak, and I was seeing just how this was going to happen here at the RCF. The people in charge of this place were as out of control as the command at Fort Stewart. They would not hesitate to use their position of authority to berate and belittle the inmates in the facility. Some of the guards were decent people, but the majority of them had some very big egos and problems with knowing how to handle their authority.

The senior enlisted man at the facility was very unsure of himself as a man and the only way he could prove to himself that he was one, was to inflict as much bullshit on the inmates as possible. I understand that prison is not supposed to be a day-care center, but when someone deliberately pushes your buttons and then wants to add time to your sentence when you stand up to him, then that person is out of line.

Army Regulation 190-47 governs how military confinement operates and it explains what is and is not allowed in the facility. The
command structure of this particular facility chose not to follow the
guidelines as often as possible. It would put on a good show when
someone came in for inspection or to investigate an allegation of
wrongdoing, but when the people doing the inspecting were gone, the
playacting was over.

One of the requirements of the regulations at the time I was
incarcerated was that no female guards were allowed to see into the
living cells where the inmates showered, used the toilet, and slept.
Females were allowed to guard male inmates while on work details
and in other parts of the prison, but not in the living areas.

This facility would constantly break this regulation by assigning
female guards to be on the tier where the inmates were housed during
the allotted time for showers, which was easily visible from where the
guards were posted. (This situation was changed shortly after a few of
us started writing letters to our elected representatives, complaining
about it.) Well, you can imagine what would happen when the male
inmates were showering and the female guards turned their eyes in
the direction of the shower areas.

This situation was used against the inmates on numerous times
to send them before the discipline and adjustment (D&A) board.
One inmate complained that the females were allowed to see into the
living areas of the tier, and as a result he was placed in what was called
the "Bravo" cell block, where an inmate would go to be punished for
infractions of the rules. (This block was sort of semi-solitary confinement. I describe it this way because you were in your own cell but
you could talk to others in the block because the cells were adjacent to
one another.) This inmate would not accept the fact that he was being
punished for talking about the facility breaking the regulations, and
he continued to speak out about it. The senior enlisted man ordered
the water turned off in the inmate's cell, and after about three days,
the cell was getting pretty rank. (You can only imagine the condition
of the cell, as it is about six feet wide and twelve feet long, with a toilet
and a bunk in it.)

The inmate was not able to flush the toilet or perform any personal
hygiene for three days, and the senior enlisted man went to the cell
block to further harass the inmate, who by this time had had enough.

The inmate reached into the toilet that had been brewing for three days and proceeded to give this individual a "taste of his own medicine," and he threw the result of three days of being unable to flush his toilet into the face of the enlisted man.

The inmate was ordered into what is known as a "restraint chair" for four days without being let out to relieve himself or for any personal hygiene. The restraint chair is a hard plastic and metal chair that puts the person in it into a very uncomfortable position, and by regulation is not supposed to be used for more than four hours. They kept this inmate in it for *four days*. This is one example of the abuse of inmates at this facility.

Monica Kevin first met with the chaplain and explained his concerns, referring him to our Web site and giving him as much information as possible. The chaplain was not very encouraging. His response was similar to the response of Kevin's battalion chaplain, telling Kevin that he did not share Kevin's beliefs regarding war. Kevin tried approaching the chaplain again, but there was little point in pursuing any assistance from the man. He was not going to cooperate. We had reached the point where we believed an army chaplain was nothing more than a mouthpiece for the chain of command, keeping the officers informed of any soldiers who might become a problem. In our personal experience, we had no feeling that the chaplains we encountered would do anything to provide real guidance or counseling to soldiers who needed their help. They were clearly unable to see past their own military indoctrination.

Kevin Getting help from the prison chaplain was not very easy, as he told me war is a good thing, in his opinion. I knew then I would have to talk to someone else who could assist me in getting the army to really consider my application for conscientious objector. Everyone has a right to his or her opinions, but it is the responsibility of the military chaplain to provide assistance and guidance to service members in spiritual matters and not to insert their own opinions into what someone else is trying to consider in his or her spiritual life.

If the chaplain believes in war, then the chaplain should fight in them, but if someone has doubts and questions about the validity of war, then the chaplain should not give an opinion. If the chaplain doesn't want to listen to a soldier who has been to war and then realizes that fighting in wars and helping train others to fight in war isn't the best thing for the soldier spiritually, then the chaplain should not hinder the person in trying to reach a place that is the best for that soldier spiritually.

Monica Kevin called to ask me for help in finding a civilian chaplain who would respect his universal faith without trying to close him into a religious box and give him an outlet to discuss his beliefs without facing retribution. From my perspective, it would be good to have someone close to the prison who would be able to visit Kevin from time to time, giving him a contact with reality and making certain he was staying strong.

Once again, we have come to know some very special people throughout this journey. Our friend, the Franciscan priest who had spent time with us during Kevin's first court-martial, knew a priest in the Seattle area who turned out to be another very good and caring man and who came to be a friend as well. I called him and explained the situation to him. He was willing to do whatever he could to help, so we initiated the approval process for his visitation with Kevin.

The approval process for outside visitors to the Fort Lewis RCF is something to wonder at. Kevin completed an application requesting a visit from the priest. It took several days for the RCF staff to return the forms, which were required to be completed by the priest before they could conduct a background check. It was Kevin's responsibility to mail the forms to the priest. This was done, the forms completed and returned. Three weeks went by and the RCF staff notified Kevin the priest had been approved for a visit. The same staff, however, called the priest to inform him that his paperwork had not been completed and he was required to submit another packet for approval. If I had not been able to act as a go-between for these two men, Kevin would not have been aware of what was happening. Kevin requested another approval packet and mailed it to the priest who completed it promptly and returned it to the RCF. Two weeks again went by and there was still no approval. The priest contacted the Fort Lewis division chaplain who informed him there should not be such difficulty in his being approved to visit Kevin. The prison command saw things differently.

We pursued this issue with several political figures in the Seattle area, explaining the circumstances and the roadblocks set in place. Within days, Kevin was called into the warden's office. The warden informed Kevin that he was not comfortable with Kevin's receiving a visit from a civilian chaplain, going so far as to suggest that Kevin might not really want the visit, that it might be my doing rather than Kevin's. After hearing that the warden would prefer that Kevin meet with the prison chaplain as opposed to a civilian chaplain, Kevin spoke up and said it was at his request that the priest be allowed to visit and it was his right to have such a visit as well. There was nothing more the warden could do, knowing this issue had now become a public issue. He finally allowed the visit after almost two months of working to prevent it.

This set the stage for the type of treatment Kevin would receive from the command of the RCF for the entire length of his stay at Fort Lewis.

September 2005—Prison Time

Kevin On July 28, 2005, the United States of America decided to send me to prison because I developed a conscience as a result of serving in the military, experiencing war firsthand and realizing that I could not participate in the wanton destruction of another country through the use of our military might. It was a war that had nothing to do with the defense of this country at any rate. Our president had designs on the mineral wealth of Iraq and he was able to convince the nation that the president of Iraq was intent on coming to America and robbing us of our freedom when, in reality, nothing could have been further from the truth.

I went to Iraq with the idea that we had to protect ourselves from the WMDs that were supposedly being produced by the ton by a madman intent on dropping them on New York, California, and Washington, DC. What I learned was that we went to a country that didn't even have a well-organized conventional army, much less hordes of specialized personnel ready to unleash Armageddon on the United States.

The truth of what war is and what it really does to people started to sink in, and I began to question what business we have, in the modern age, pursuing such an insane policy as war. What would make a man stand up and announce to the world that he wanted to go down in history as the "War President"? Are we so caught up in playing army that we refuse to look at the reality of how stupid war really is?

October 2005

Monica I thought about the military, the soldiers, the chaplains, and the role of religion in the circle they all composed. The military chaplains we came in contact with seemed controlled by the officers in command. They all seemed to want to touch on spiritual issues, and many did so in editorials written for installation newspapers, and by giving sermons on Sundays. None seemed to have the latitude for dealing with the reality of the spirit of soldiers, however, and none we met seemed prepared to deal with real questions of conscience or the emotional turmoil many combat veterans faced because of their conscience.

I cannot speak about the actions of every military chaplain, and it would be wrong for me to characterize them all as the few we encountered. It would be no different than with any group of people we have worked with in our lives. Kevin was faced with a chain of command in his company that showed very little integrity or respect for the humanity of the soldiers they were commissioned to lead, but that by no means was representative of every commander in the U.S. military. We also have been given tremendous assistance by officers in the army who *did* care about their soldiers, and who cared enough about their own standards to want to maintain them with integrity.

The chaplains we met, with the exception of one man, all seemed to have been given a handbook for chaplaincy and practiced the art by rote, according to the written guidelines the military established for dealing with religion and soldiers.

I personally don't believe the military chaplains would be able to address real moral issues from a perspective other than one the military hierarchy established, unless they were prepared to face their own conscience first. From what I witnessed, military chaplains must find a way to deceive themselves, whether knowingly or not, as much as the military must use its training methods to deceive soldiers into believing they do not have to question the morality of their actions. Kevin faced his conscience head-on, and the chaplains he approached for guidance in his conscientious objector application were not prepared to answer the questions he was asking. They did not want to have to answer those questions, it seemed. It was easier to turn away, to write one more soldier's morality off to fear, cowardice, "lack of moral fortitude," than to face themselves and find their own responses to his questions to be something they did not want to hear.

Midway through Kevin's sentence at the military prison, construction was under way on Fort Stewart. Just down the road from the main gate, and within view of the new headquarters building being constructed simultaneously, a brand new chapel complex was taking shape. It didn't matter how many times I drove through the main gate, I was still struck by the complexity of the issue of morality, the question of religion, and the existence of the new chapel structure on a military installation while my husband was serving time in prison for facing his moral questions head-on and deciding his conscience required him to move in a new direction.

Not long after the incident with the civilian chaplain's visitation approval at the Fort Lewis RCF, I drove past the chapel complex on Fort Stewart. Laying there on the ground in front of this huge structure designed to meet the spiritual needs of more than twenty thousand soldiers and their families, was its brilliant white steeple. I recalled watching as a tree was decorated for Christmas; first the lights, then the ornaments, and the final touch, the star at the peak that signaled the transformation from pine tree to holiday spirit. I thought about the steeple lying on its side before the incomplete chapel complex for this military installation and wondered, "Would the transformation from an ordinary, redbrick building to a spiritual center for soldiers' lives be complete when the steeple was added as the final touch?" Somehow I think not.

There is so much more to a person's spirit than can be covered in a chaplain's instruction manual. There is far more to the conscience of a soldier who faces the questions that combat draws forth than any chaplain can address, unless that chaplain is willing to face the same questions for himself. I do not believe the building of a chapel complex is going to fill the needs of the soldiers who will be returning from war. I do not believe there can be a manual to prepare anyone, nor can there be study groups or movies recalling wars of the past or coffeehouses designed for soldiers to share thoughts that can satisfactorily address the questions of conscience our soldiers and their families will face.

I believe the answer lies in a different place with a different solution. Conscience is the part of every person that has the potential to guide someone's actions and lead that person in the right direction. When conscience is suppressed, when it is blocked and not acknowledged, that person becomes a person easily led, a follower. When we do not allow ourselves to listen to our conscience, it is easy to be misled by the misrepresentations of those who would act, thinking only of themselves. True people of conscience cannot be led, nor would they believe they had a right to lead others. People of conscience have walked a long road on their own and find peace in knowing that they could take that path without others along, facing every obstacle put before them by those who wanted to see them fail.

October 2005

Kevin I have been talking with some of the other guys who are in the RCF with me, and there are about three or four who have been charged with murder for doing what their commanders told them to do. One inmate is twenty-two years old, and his squad leader told him to shoot an unarmed Iraqi just because they had found an AK-47 Russian assault rifle in the man's house.

This young soldier was sent to war, and he went proudly, believing he was doing the right thing. He faithfully followed orders from the squad leader (usually a staff sergeant), and as a result, a military judge charged him with murder and sentenced him to five years in prison.

Something is wrong with an organization that trains you to follow all the orders given to you without question, and then puts you in prison when you do. As a contrast, I refused to follow orders that were in violation of our laws—the Nuremberg Tribunal, Geneva Conventions, and our Constitution—and I was sent to prison as well. How do you deal with an organization that has no method for understanding how it wants soldiers to behave? The hypocrisy is at an amazing level, because you are damned if you do and damned if you don't.

November 2005

Monica It wasn't easy with Kevin three thousand miles away in a military prison that controlled every aspect of his life, including the contact he had with me. It was frustrating to know that he was not telling me everything he had to deal with during his time at Fort Lewis, but I knew he was doing it to make things easier for me. I did my best to do the same for him. He was facing a very difficult situation, and it was not of his doing. I knew that he had plenty of time on his hands at the RCF, and I also knew he would spend some of it thinking about the situation he felt responsible for putting me in. He was not responsible, but I knew he would have moments of feeling that way.

He had chosen what he believed to be best for him and for his family. His command, a command that had a commitment to see that the needs of its soldiers were met, was not strong enough to act as men, choosing to punish Kevin for pointing out its weaknesses. I chose to do what I could to support Kevin. I chose. I was determined to see that the life Kevin had worked so hard for was not lost while he was in prison. I wrote a letter to him every morning and did what I could to ensure that I was available whenever it was possible for him to call.

Almost daily I remembered the time he had served in Iraq and was struck by the similarity of the emotions, concerns, and effects of this different kind of deployment. I found myself maintaining as many habits as possible. I kept everything the same and included parts of our life in the letters I wrote. It was important to both of us to maintain that sense of connection to our life together. It was as if time stopped while he was gone, and we simply went through the motions, changing as little as possible so that we could start again right where we left off when he returned home. I even left a pile of clean clothes belonging to Kevin in a chair near his dresser, laughing when I told him he was going to have to put them all away when he got home. It seemed to be the little things that kept us going, mundane routines that kept us in touch with what we would get back to as soon as the madness was over. Sometimes people became frustrated with me because I would not do anything that was going to alter our routine as long as Kevin was in prison unjustly.

I spent a great deal of time doing what I could to bring attention to Kevin's case. The people who supported us cared about what was happening. I wanted to make sure there were updates and information about Kevin as a way of showing them we cared about them as well.

At this point we relied on donations from those who believed in Kevin's position regarding war and who believed he had been treated unjustly by the army. Kevin's sentence had included loss of pay in addition to the prison sentence and a dishonorable discharge. The people who gave such generous support during this very challenging time meant more to us than the money they gave. It was important to us that they knew this. Kevin and I have what we need, and while it is modest, it is what we worked for together, and I was going to do everything I could to make sure we did not lose it because of the manipulations and intimidation by a command that couldn't care less about anyone's humanity, let alone Kevin's.

I chose not to become publicly involved in the large network of antiwar organizations. We appreciated their help in drawing attention to Kevin's case when it first became public knowledge, but Kevin and I did not feel comfortable with many of the organizations that claimed to have the soldiers' best interests at heart, and yet whose agenda seemed to become increasingly directed away from the needs of the soldiers and toward politics and foreign policy. For me, it became a double-edged sword. We were running out of options as far as seeing that our bills were paid. I know that if I had attended rallies, protests, and speaking events sponsored by many of these groups, it would have been easier from a fund-raising standpoint, but the methods they were using went against what Kevin and I believed, and we did not want our message to be lost in the process.

I eventually found part-time work and spent the rest of the time writing articles about conscientious objection and working with attorneys, alternative media writers, and congressional representatives to see that Kevin was treated fairly and that his case was given the consideration it was due.

There were many people who gave, individuals who in many instances became very good friends. We cared for them in ways they may not have understood, although we hoped they might. Veterans gave more than they had a right to, far more than we expected, and we assured them they would not be forgotten. We may not ever be able to directly thank each of them, but we will do what we can to help others, and we will do it in the name of those who were so generous to us when we needed them to be. This was one benefit of not allowing ourselves to be caught up in the swift current of a movement that soon lost sight of the humanity of its thousands of participants. By staying focused on our relationship, our situation, and doing as much as we could ourselves to maintain public awareness of Kevin's case, we were able to maintain contact with the humanity of those who supported our actions, as well as with our own.

November 2005

Monica I had considered the possibility of flying to Seattle to spend Thanksgiving Day with Kevin. He had called and said there was to be a special dinner at the facility, and family members were allowed to attend. It had required a great deal of pressure from congressional offices and other public figures in order to even hear from the command of the RCF at all. I submitted my request to be approved for visitation, something that frustrated me to begin with. The army knew very well who I was; I should not have been required to go through an approval process to visit Kevin. I waited several weeks for a response from the staff at the RCF, to no avail, and the calls I made to the RCF simply went unanswered.

Kevin pursued the issue from within the RCF as the holiday approached and time became a factor. We were at the point where we trusted no one in a command position in any part of the army. After the actions of the chain of command of Kevin's company, we were gun-shy when it came to trusting the word of anyone in a position to make any decisions in the army. I do not believe that every person we dealt with was corrupt or had negative intent. I believe that many simply had their hands tied by a system that was being directed by those who chose not to follow the rules, laying the groundwork for deception and lies in an effort to cover their actions. Those at the lower levels of the command were not in a position to override the faulty practices of their "superior" officers. I believe incompetence was also a factor in precipitating the need to cover up personal actions of those in charge. They simply didn't know the regulations and made no effort to learn them, choosing instead to make them up as they went along. Rather than lead by good example, these commanders then bullied their subordinates using their rank as leverage until no one was sure what the regulations were any longer.

A first sergeant at the RCF seemed to understand our situation and did what he could to help us with the visitation issue. Finally, by working with him directly, I was able to have my visit approved, but it was the day before Thanksgiving (I wondered if the powers that be had planned it that way) and far too late to find a flight and make arrangements with friends. I was frustrated, but knew it was one more instance of some member of the command being afraid of the message of Kevin's position, and I chalked it up to moral weakness of men who, in a position to make a difference, chose to make the wrong difference. We would get through this, too; we were stronger than they wanted us to be, even thousands of miles apart.

I had reached another point of frustration. I knew Kevin was facing many more attempts at intimidation from the staff at the RCF than he would tell me. I could hear it in his voice when he called. I made sure I was near the phone every night, and as expensive as the phone calls were, I cut corners everywhere I could to make sure there was always money available for him to make those calls. I didn't need to know the specifics of the treatment he was receiving to know that there were times when he would have liked to lose control with those who held him captive. I was even more aware of the fact that those who were pushing him out there would have loved the opportunity to put Kevin through another court-martial for losing control with one of them. I was not going to close the last connection to humanity that Kevin had. I would not give those who were out to break Kevin the chance to do so.

With the help of another very good person with knowledge of computer language, we set up a new Web site devoted to the legal aspects of Kevin's case and its chronology (http://www.BendermanTimeline. com). We hoped this site would be informative and serve to instruct those who spent time on it in the ways of a military organization whose commanders were not held accountable to the regulations or their oath to serve. We hoped those in the military service who were facing their own battles with their chain of command would see they were not alone, and continue to stand strong against what was being done. We believed that by standing for justice—using the system of justice as it was intended—eventually, the tide would turn if enough soldiers were willing to stand with us. We received responses from over six hundred members of the military in the course of the two years Kevin's case was public. All of them faced their own injustice during their time of service. We could not solve their problems for them, but we could give them resources and ideas about how to proceed to help themselves.

I watched the news and reported as much as I could to Kevin. It was clear things were not going well in Iraq, and we heard from many soldiers here at home who were frustrated with the situation, with their involvement, and no end in sight. I again became angry, and wrote another letter. This time it was my version of a letter to the president, and after it was published I realized it had been written one year to the day from the date Kevin had written a letter of his own to the president to start this public message of the need to end war—all war.

• • •

Monica's Letter to President George Bush— November 20, 2005

Dear Mr. Bush—
Over one year ago, my husband showed the integrity of a true leader by facing everything he had committed to for you, in the name of—well, first there was national security, then it was freedom from tyranny for the Iraqis, then it was terrorism, then it was freedom for the American people, and what is it now? Don't worry—we know. It hasn't changed. First it was oil, and then it was saving face for a president who has never faced responsibility for his actions—*ever*. But now, you are a president who has nowhere left to hide—you've seen for yourself, the doors are locked, you cannot escape us.

You and your army of commanders could not allow my husband to have his voice—you actually thought you could control him—and the *truth* he had to speak. You put him in prison and thought you could take him away from me. You dared to believe we would go away quietly and leave you to your war.

Your army cannot control him, because the truth will not hide. And the commitment my husband made to defend the Constitution, to keep his soldiers safe—and to defend his home and his family—has a depth of integrity you will never understand.

Your doors are locking around you, Sir. And the jail cell that you put my husband in—the prison that confines all of our soldiers—this war and the horrific actions you have asked them to commit in our country's name—their doors are opening. I hope you feel every moment of this—and, Sir, I hope you know it comes from Kevin and me.

For over a year, my husband, Sgt. Kevin Benderman, took everything the military could pound him with and walked tall, held his head high—knowing the day would come when the "truth would set him free." I walk every step with him, Sir—not to hold him up when his drugged stupor wears off, no, Sir—I walk proudly by my husband's side, because I know the leader he is, and I know the strength that he has. It is an honor, Sir—to stand by his side and help him build his case against you and all of those who have dared to disrespect him.

What is it that you and the commanders who imprisoned him are so afraid of?

Why was it that they were so willing to commit crimes, to tell lies, and to manipulate evidence in my husband's case?

Because they have known from the beginning that he speaks the truth—and my husband's voice is a powerful voice. They should be afraid—you should be afraid—very, very afraid.

You dared to use this country to give yourself a place in history. You dared to use my husband's integrity, his honor, and his commitment to duty, and thought that his dignity could somehow serve to make you great.

You were wrong, Sir.

One year ago, my husband told the world what he knew to be true. Attorneys, advisors told him it would be difficult to prove.

Kevin and I knew better—and I stood beside him knowing we would face what you and your commanders would try to do, together, and in time, *you* would prove what he already knew. That is what happens with the truth. He knew this—because he lives this—a powerful man.

You, Sir—wouldn't know the truth if it looked you in the eye. *Ahhh*—I'm wrong—you know the truth and it terrifies you.

Those locked doors in Korea—they are the end of your road—there is no one to help you, and what you thought you had locked away is your worst nightmare now.

My husband will not be silenced—for he speaks the truth, and it is coming for you.

Monica Benderman

• • •

November 2005—Foundation for Peace

Kevin We all have to work together to build a solid foundation of peace in this world. We have to build this foundation using bricks from all over the world, meaning people from every country who will be doing their part to build a lasting peace.

I know that everyone laying down their weapons and extending their hands to close the divide among people is the only way, and learning about the other people we share this planet with, ridding ourselves of ignorance, is the way to accomplish this.

I went to war believing that the people we were going to be killing were out to kill us. After I was there and started talking to the people, I realized that we have more in common than some would want us to believe. Not all of those people are raving, bloodthirsty, and crazed madmen.

The picture that was painted for me of these people was a group of bloodthirsty savages, but the truth is far different. I met people just like those I know here at home: construction workers, engineers, schoolteachers, and so forth. Some were Arabs, some were Kurds, some Sunnis, some Shias, and they all wanted the same thing: They all wanted to be secure in their homes and to earn a living. That is when I realized that I could not, in good conscience, kill any of these people.

I am going to spend the rest of my life laying as many bricks on the foundation of peace throughout the world as I possibly can. Will you work with me?

December 2005

Monica When Kevin first arrived at the RCF in Fort Lewis, in addition to requesting a meeting with the chaplain, he also asked to have contact with his military defense attorney. This should have been an easy request to fulfill. Kevin was entitled to confidential communications with his attorney—it was the law. His attorney was a major in the U.S. Army and the senior defense counsel at Fort Stewart. He would be handling the post-trial paperwork, and ensuring that everything was done correctly so that Kevin could initiate the appeal of his case as quickly as possible. Kevin submitted his request in writing, and for the next three months was given every excuse possible, with every roadblock the RCF staff could dream up to prevent him from having access to his attorney, as was his right.

Kevin was required to give the RCF a list of the attorneys he requested contact with. In addition to his military defense counsel, he listed a second attorney who had also been involved in Kevin's courts-martial. This man was the gentleman who had invited us to participate in the peace rally in Youngstown, Ohio, marking the second anniversary of the invasion of Iraq. He had prepared an amicus curiae brief on Kevin's behalf, with a strong justification for Kevin's decision to file a conscientious objector application in opposition to war. The amicus brief had been filed with the judge presiding over Kevin's second court-martial but had not been argued in court. Kevin wanted to remain in contact with this man, both for advice regarding his conscientious objector application and the legal process and as a friend.

Both attorneys were shown to have represented Kevin in his record of trial (verbatim transcripts of the court-martial proceedings); however, the RCF made it very difficult for Kevin to have any contact with either of them. The military defense counsel finally contacted me and informed me of the difficulty he was having in reaching Kevin. This struck me as odd. He said he was unable to reach anyone by telephone, and the deadline for filing Kevin's post-trial motions and recommendations was at hand. He felt the best way for him to have contact with Kevin was for Kevin to initiate the action from within the RCF. Once again it became necessary to involve congressional representatives and other public officials before the RCF staff was willing to follow regulations and respond to Kevin's request.

Days after Kevin's sole communication with his defense attorney, and before he was able to submit a final statement on his own behalf for the post-trial record, the convening authority at Fort Stewart completed his review that was begun after Kevin's sentence was handed down in July. His final decision was to allow the conviction and sentence of the court-martial to stand as the judge had written it. We had expected nothing different. The months of pressure from as many directions as we could apply was not so much to influence the convening authority to change the sentence but to have him sign off on it in a timely manner so Kevin could begin the appeal process. The convening authority at Fort Stewart had a history of delaying its decision for as long as possible in cases similar to Kevin's. There were instances in which the final decision of the convening authority had not been made until after soldiers had served their complete sentence. We were certain it was the intent of the convening authority to do the same in Kevin's case. We knew his case would most likely have to go to the appellate courts for justice, but we did not want the convening authority to have the opportunity to exert any more control over the case than he already had.

Even before the investigation into the bogus charges that were finally presented before the court by the command at Fort Stewart, the convening authority had violated regulations of military justice. In the record of trial for Kevin's courts-martial, evidence demonstrated the convening authority's bias in Kevin's case and showed his willingness to use his rank against the regulations in order to discipline Kevin for telling the truth about conditions at Fort Stewart. In a meeting with prosecutors prior to the first Article 32 hearing in Kevin's case, it became clear the convening authority was going to settle for nothing less than Kevin's going to jail. In documentation filed by Kevin's defense attorney, it was shown that the convening authority exhibited "Undue Command Influence" by telling the prosecution that he would accept nothing less than a sentence of eighteen months in prison as an outcome in Kevin's case. This alone should have been enough to have Kevin's case dismissed, as there had yet to be any evidence presented to justify any charges being filed, let alone proving Kevin's guilt. It became clear to us that, in military justice, justice is not always determined by the regulations and a soldier's rights. The convening authority in Kevin's case embodies the reason why we have come to be very untrusting of military officers and military justice, as he chose to manipulate evidence and testimony, and ultimately decide against Kevin as a personal vendetta rather than making a fair, impartial judgment.

As much as I would have liked to spend the Christmas holidays in Seattle to visit Kevin, we had to make another choice. Money was the issue; it wouldn't do much good to have spent time with Kevin if our bills were not paid and he did not have a home to return to when his sentence had been served.

At this point we still believed it would be best to have a civilian defense attorney work with the military appellate attorney on Kevin's appeal. We still had little trust in the officers detailed to the legal defense division of the army. We did not necessarily believe that every officer was unethical, but the system itself had become one in which those who were unethical could exercise their influence over the system with little accountability to justice in the process. We believed that having a civilian attorney working alongside the military would help hold the system accountable to its own regulations. This, however, also meant more money was needed. Civilian attorneys were not cheap, and most of those we spoke with were willing to help but not until we were able to raise enough money to cover a $15,000 retainer. Kevin was a soldier and had been sentenced to fifteen months' confinement with loss of pay. We realized that attorneys should not be expected to work for free, but something about this did not sit well. Soldiers went to war, putting their lives on the line to defend our laws. Kevin had come to terms with the fact that his service was not in defense of those laws and could no longer allow his moral principles to be abused by the hypocrisy of what he had been asked to do. In making this choice, he once again put his life on the line to defend our nation's laws, and the laws of humanity, and yet it was becoming increasingly difficult to find anyone willing to defend Kevin with the same commitment to principle.

Christmas passed quietly. I was able to mail a package of treats to Kevin. It reminded me again of the first time war put so much physical distance between us. I mailed lots of cards and letters, extra for the holidays, and was grateful to learn that many of the people who supported his actions had done the same.

Once Kevin had become more familiar with the routine and regulations of the RCF, I posted his mailing address on several Web sites so that those who wished to send him letters of support would be able to. Kevin would not be able to read all the messages of support until he returned home. The military prison had strict guidelines regarding mail. Kevin was able to receive mail from the people he specified on a mailing list. The RCF staff monitored the mail he received, reading all of it before he could. When Kevin first arrived and mail was sent with addresses not listed on his approved list, the RCF simply returned the mail to the sender marked "Refused." After more calls from congressional offices, and realizing the amount of mail coming into the RCF from all over the world for Kevin, the RCF command made arrangements for Kevin to forward to our home all the mail from addresses not approved rather than letting the staff take the time to return it.

The amount of cards and letters we received was beyond belief. In addition to mail being sent to Kevin, we continued to receive an incredible amount of mail here at home. Most astounding were the hundreds of handmade holiday cards from students of every school in Quebec and the Netherlands. I had never stopped to realize just how far word of Kevin's message had traveled. We would have liked to have responded to every student who wrote; we hoped our actions would speak for us.

We continued to consider everything we did very carefully before responding to any of the issues created by the military. We knew how many people were watching us, and we wanted to be clear about the message we sent. We believe in taking steps to bring about change, but we hoped the change would be positive and move us all a little closer to the peace so many spoke of. All around us we heard those who were angry at the administration, seeking vengeance for what was believed to be illegal acts, and the talk was negative, always negative.

We wanted no part in negative acts. The situation we were in was the result of our response to negative actions against soldiers on the part of military command, and in turn the decisions made by the administration. We saw nothing good in attacking what had been done with angry reaction. We carefully considered every step we took so that, hopefully, we were always moving forward toward a positive resolution, and when it came time to look back, we could do so with no regret.

• • •

Thoughts on Christmas Day

Kevin and I spoke often during the holiday. The phone lines for the inmates were open and we had a great deal to think about. We shared our thoughts with the people who visited our Web site:

What Have We Learned?

Christmas comes but once a year. Why? Maybe it is a reminder.

Churches are full on Christmas Eve. So many pay homage, listening to the story of Christmas. Year after year, children memorize the Christmas story, learn to point in the direction of the Star of Bethlehem, and surround a cradle full of hay to sing "Away in a Manger," with hands folded sweetly to their chins.

The children grow and remember Christmases past as they watch their own child's hands wrapped gently around the flickering light of one candle as "Silent Night" is softly echoed in a darkened sanctuary.

What have we learned?

A baby was born long ago, in a manger full of hay. His parents were not rich, but they loved each other and they loved their child. He was a child of God, a gift. God knew this couple would love their child, and so He trusted them to raise him well. This child grew, and lived his life the best he could. He learned from great teachers, and he walked the earth because he lived at a time when there was little other form of conveyance for a man of meager means. He loved, for he understood. He taught what he had learned, to all who would listen. He was a man of peace, for he knew that in the quiet of peace, the answers come. He understood that not all men saw as he did, and he was patient. He listened, and heard their fears; he watched them live and knew that if he could somehow show them not to be afraid, they, too, would find the peace he knew so well.

Men followed him, for they wanted what he had. Men revered him for the gifts he gave, and raised him to lofty heights, for surely no man except a man of God could be so patient, so understanding, so kind, and so wise. Men praised him, and wrote stories about him. Before long, he was a hero. Everywhere he traveled people knew his name and glorified him, and as the story grew, so did the image, but the man remained the same. He knew who he was. Just a man.

In time, he began to believe the stories, and he began to believe the power the stories gave through the idolatry of the men who followed him. When he needed it most, the peace he had felt, the patience that it offered, seemed to disappear and he too, became afraid. But in the silence that nature and time alone can give, he found himself again and knew that what was in his heart had never left him—it was he who had chosen not to see.

Humility returned as he remembered the gifts were only there as long as he realized in whose name they had been given.

Men feared him for the peace that surrounded him. Powerful men wanted to destroy him, for those who followed him seemed strengthened, and would not blindly follow the leaders of the day. The sins of man led to this man's death. Fear— because this man lived in peace, and those who followed him did so without being threatened, coerced, or bought. They followed him simply because he accepted them, walked with them, held their hands and listened—even when their differences were disfiguring, when they spoke in different languages, when they practiced different customs.

Somewhere tonight a child will be born. To his parents, this child will be a gift from God. A demonstration of God's trust in them to raise the child well, to teach him to live in peace and to raise him to walk among men with humility, patience, and consideration for all.

How is this child different than the one we honor in the manger? He is no different. He will have the same gifts given, and the same hopes shared. He will begin his life in the same simple way that all children do.

This child will be given teachers; he will have the opportunity to learn as he grows, and the chance to practice peace in his life.

He will be influenced by his world. Will it be a world of peace, a world where he can find the silence in which to learn to listen to his heart?

Will it be a world that will allow him to understand what he is given, and how to use these gifts? Will it be a world where he is accepted for who he is—someone who cares, who listens, who holds hands with those who are disfigured, or speak different languages, or practice different customs?

Will he learn the wisdom of moral courage when faced with threats from people who fear him?

If he does, will he be seen as an idol, someone to be revered and honored, someone elevated to such a standard that others will see him as a savior rather than just a man with enough faith in himself to live by his own beliefs? Will people look at his actions and his life and walk away, afraid of what he is and the standard that he sets?

Will he remain strong in his principles, and humbled by the life he has been given?

Or will he forget where his gifts came from, and let the love of power, money, and fame interfere with the peace in his heart, and cause him to forget who he really is? Will his love of external trappings overshadow the real gifts, so that he becomes defensive and untrusting of anyone who does not think as he does? Will he allow material gains to define him, so that he lives in fear of their loss unmasking the shallow illusion of a man? Will he reach for security in the form of guns, chemical weapons, war— destroying anyone who threatens to reveal his weaknesses?

Every child born is no different than the child in the manger.

What have we learned?

•   •   •

January 2006

Monica Kevin's sentence was for more than one year; therefore, he was eligible to be considered for parole after serving six months. This meant he would be eligible to be released on parole on January 27, 2006. According to military regulations governing prison facilities and inmate rights, Kevin's parole board hearing was to be scheduled for no later than thirty days prior to his eligibility date. Kevin had been told in November that he had until the end of that month to submit his paperwork requesting parole to the RCF parole counselor. The counselor also informed him that he had a right to ask anyone he chose to write a letter of support and recommendation to be included in his parole packet, and these letters should also be received by the counselor's office before the end of November. All of this was done, and many good people wrote letters on Kevin's behalf. December came and went and Kevin learned that his parole board hearing had been scheduled for February 15, 2006, clearly a violation of the regulations. There didn't seem to be anything anyone could do to change it. Once again we learned how unjust the military justice system is as long as those in command do not feel pressure from anyone willing to hold them accountable.

Reluctantly, we searched for a civilian attorney to assist Kevin with his parole hearing. He would not be able to be present at the hearing, but he would be able to help Kevin with his paperwork. We also felt that there would be a measure of fairness in the treatment of Kevin's case if those on the parole board knew an attorney was participating. It did not make one bit of difference. Kevin went through the same games to have the new attorney listed on his approved list as he had faced with the priest, his military attorney, myself, and others. It didn't matter what Kevin requested; the RCF staff did their best to make things as difficult as possible for him.

I continued to write articles about conscientious objection, Kevin's and my feelings about war and peace, and the need to seek a positive resolution to the issues our country faced. No matter what Web site I visited or what media resource I used, there was little in the way of anything positive being written. Now, having been fully immersed in the war, knowing soldiers who had lost their lives, families who faced the loss and continued deployments, and having a husband unjustly serving time for exercising his rights to declare himself a conscientious objector and live by his own principles of morality, I was well aware of the seriousness of the current situation our country was in. I remain aware. My firsthand experiences have taught me that we cannot lose hope if we are to continue to move toward an end to the destruction and chaos that a situation as negative as war creates. I felt those in the military would continue to apply as much pressure as possible on Kevin and me until they were able to break our resolve to live with hope and continue to seek resolution to the situation caused by the lack of integrity on the part of so many members of the command. Things became very difficult at times, but I loved Kevin, and that mattered enough to make me want to keep going. He had done nothing wrong. He had walked to the van that took him to jail with his head held high. He had his integrity and his principles intact. We were going to get through this together, and we were going to win.

Some days when Kevin called I could tell things had been rough. Other days his calls were just what I needed to keep me going. We did what we could to keep each other strong, and it was worth it. The army did not deserve to see us break, and we would not give them the opportunity to believe their methods would succeed.

Our congressional representative was very supportive and assigned an experienced caseworker to be available whenever we needed help from her office. He had been a counselor during the Vietnam war and understood the psychological games the military could play as it tried to break a defiant soldier. This man is a good friend now, and he has done more than anyone to help us stand strong against the unjust actions of Kevin's commanders and the staff at the RCF. He has been a tremendous resource for historical information regarding military law and precedents, and together we have had many discussions on the need for reform in the military.

Kevin and I do not believe it is time to consider disbanding the military, as some vocal peace activists advocate. That is simply an irrational discussion to have from our perspective. There are still reasons to maintain a strong military, in our opinion, but one that is held accountable to the law and is meant as a peacekeeping force rather than an aggressive one. The world is unstable, and innocent people have the right to expect someone to step in to defend them if needed. The military should be trained and prepared to act if such a need arises, but as peacekeepers, as defenders of the peace, not as mercenaries sent to war at the whim of a government administration seeking to put its name in the annals of history as saviors of freedom and democracy in countries that have not asked for our help. The caseworker assigned to help us with Kevin's situation understood our position more than most. Over time we have had countless discussions on soldiers' rights, democracy in the military, and selective conscientious objection, all of which in combination would create greater restrictions on a government's ability to send our military personnel to war without just cause.

Our discussions led to more writing. I did what I could to maintain publicity for Kevin's case, and this angered the command. I believe one reason Kevin was sent three thousand miles away to serve his time was to put distance between us in the hope that our communication with the public would be controlled. The army really didn't take the time to understand; we had nothing to hide and we were telling the truth. There was little reason for us to fear the threats it made or the intimidation it applied. The more we spoke, the greater the intimidation became, and rather than shut us down, Kevin's commanders simply brought more attention to themselves and their fear of what we might say.

Kevin continued to write letters to post on our Web site. There was nothing the army could do about them, either. Kevin was not speaking with contempt, nor was he directing his comments toward the actions of any one person. He simply continued to express his feelings about war and send his message regarding conscientious objection, and the fact that the need for public discussion on a new, positive level was growing stronger.

The more Kevin posted on the Web and the more I wrote, the greater the frustration of the RCF staff—or so it seemed. We had reason to believe they were receiving a great deal of public communication regarding statements from Kevin and me, as well as from investigative articles written by several alternative media journalists. The RCF command did what it could to interfere with Kevin's ability to communicate with me. The command took it a step further and dared to attempt to interfere with Kevin's ability to communicate with our congressional representative. This was a clear violation of Kevin's constitutional rights and military regulations. After several attempts at trying to contact our representative's office, Kevin contacted me and asked that I inform the caseworker what the RCF command was doing. Once again it took pressure from our congressional representative, but in the end the RCF staff was forced to comply with regulations and the Constitution.

From that point on, Kevin was able to have privileged communications with congressional offices, much to the chagrin of the RCF command. This made the prison commanders more defensive, cautious, and greatly concerned over what was being communicated to the congresswoman that they were not aware of. It was rather comical. If they were following regulations, there should have been nothing to worry about. The fact that they went to so much trouble to prevent Kevin from any type of communication with this office spoke volumes without their saying anything specific. It was all we needed to give us strength to keep moving forward, and there were times when the pressure we applied actually became enjoyable, knowing the squirming it was causing.

February 2006—Parole Hearing

Monica Kevin's parole board hearing was held on February 15. When asking people to write letters on Kevin's behalf to submit as part of the parole packet, I had also asked that they send copies to me of what they had written. It was not that I was concerned with what they would write; I wanted to be able to create my own packet of letters and information so Kevin would be able to verify that everything that was supposed to be forwarded to the Department of the Army was sent. I mailed a completed version of my packet to Kevin shortly before the hearing so the RCF staff knew we were on top of things. Kevin said I would be receiving information from the parole board detailing steps I could take to provide verbal testimony on Kevin's behalf, which would then be included for consideration by the parole board before making its final decision. I never received any information from the parole board, even after calling the board's office in Virginia to ask that the information be sent to me.

Nothing was easy, but we kept going. We had no expectations regarding the decision of the parole board. We had been through this before, many times. Perhaps if Kevin had simply served his time, and if I had quietly gone about our family's business without creating Web sites, calling congressional offices, contacting attorneys, and making sure Kevin had people contacting him, things might have turned out differently. We will never know. Neither Kevin nor I are people who sit and let others take advantage of us, or of those who are not able to stand up for themselves. We did what we did because it was right, and we will continue to move forward by listening to our conscience and making decisions based on what we believe to be the right choice.

March 2006

Monica Inmates at Fort Lewis soon learned who Kevin was and why he was serving time there. They took notice of all the mail Kevin received, and several of the local papers had published articles about Kevin, informing the communities that he was serving his time at their military installation. Several inmates had subscriptions to these newspapers and word spread. The comments and support matched what we had received from the beginning. There were a few negative comments from the guards, and naturally, the command was biased. A great number of soldiers serving as guards at the RCF quietly shared their support with Kevin, understanding the truth of what he had been saying and the reasons for what he was doing. In time, many of the guards admitted Kevin was being treated unjustly, knowing that he was being singled out for intimidation at the RCF in light of the statements he and I were making that were bringing greater attention to the actions of the command.

The inmates came to understand that Kevin had connections they did not, and soon a number of them were asking Kevin to assist them with their own situations. The conditions at the RCF were deplorable, and many of the inmates had written to congressional representatives and other organizations, trying to get help in making changes to the facility, all to no avail. Kevin was able to gather a great deal of information and have it sent to our congressional representative's office because of the pressure applied on the RCF command, ensuring that Kevin's right to privileged communications with his congresswoman was respected.

As issues from the RCF surfaced in public forums, and as congressional inquiries became a matter of course over the months Kevin remained at the RCF, the command and RCF staff demonstrated their discomfort at the questioning and the potential risk the gathering of this information represented. Clearly the command was frustrated by the fact it could not stop Kevin from addressing the concerns he and the other inmates had with the facility, or with the manner in which their individual cases were being handled.

The RCF staff was required to follow military regulations governing the operation of military prisons, but the command chose liberal interpretations of those regulations, and in many instances rewrote its own version to cover its actions and allow for discipline to meet its needs as opposed to following federal guidelines.

The inmates were expected to follow orders given by the guards without question. Kevin knew the regulations governing the facility as well as he had known the regulations governing the army. He often found guards and members of the command barking orders in reference to regulations that did not exist, made no sense, and clearly were for intimidation and no other reason. He followed orders he knew to be true; he followed orders that made sense and were in compliance with the existing military regulations. As he had done with his company command at Fort Stewart, Kevin questioned orders he knew were in violation of his rights and federal regulations governing treatment of prison inmates. He documented everything the command did and his questioning of their actions, sending copies of this documentation to the caseworker in our congressional representative's office. The RCF staff knew Kevin was doing this, but there was little they could do. They were not certain what Kevin was forwarding to the caseworker, and they could not remember the truth of every situation because they had not acted with any commitment to the truth to begin with. They began writing memos to cover their actions, postdating the memos, and documenting actions with conflicting accounts.

When an inmate violated an order, the RCF staff had the latitude to issue what was referred to as a discipline and adjustment report. It was basically a counseling statement that was forwarded to the warden's office. The warden could then order a discipline and adjustment review if he felt the inmate's actions warranted further discipline. The review could be either a one-man board to determine additional disciplinary action, or a three-man board, which was the more serious of the two.

After several months of Kevin's sending documented evidence of the conditions at the RCF, as well as instances of violations by the command, he was issued a discipline and adjustment report for a trivial order: not standing at attention quickly enough at the time of an inspection of the bay he was assigned to. The warden's response was to set up a one-man board with the warden serving as the board member, and Kevin was ordered to spend thirty days in a loss of privilege bay.

It was clear—the warden's purpose was to put Kevin in a position where he would not be able to communicate with me, and he would have great difficulty communicating with the general population of inmates, thereby cutting down on the extent of information he could forward to the congressional office. It might also prevent him from being able to forward the weekly letters he had been writing for posting on our Web site. Some guards saw what the command was doing and why, and Kevin managed to continue his contact and his letters with a little help from some friends.

April 2006

Monica We had pretty much come to terms with the fact that Kevin would serve his entire sentence. We did not expect anything from the army, and a release that came any earlier than October 2006 would be a welcome surprise.

I stayed in contact with our congressional representative's office and with others from the district Fort Lewis was in. About the time Kevin had been taken to Fort Lewis, we came in contact with the owner/editor of a relatively new alternative news site on the Internet.

He and many of those working with him were Vietnam veterans and knew full well what Kevin was dealing with. He began publishing the articles I was writing, as well as the letters Kevin was sending from Fort Lewis. Like others we had met who shared a deep understanding of the message Kevin was trying to send and the reality of what soldiers and veterans faced, he became a good friend over the course of our working together. He and the caseworker from our congressional office were the two people we trusted to understand how we wanted Kevin's case handled, including publicity. It was not our goal to become rich and famous, to have supporters pay our way to travel around the world as if we were poster children for peace, or to take advantage of the stories of soldiers and veterans as a way to wend our way into the pages of history as saviors of world peace.

Kevin and I wanted justice for Kevin's case, and in the process we hoped to use any notoriety our work gathered to bring attention to the weaknesses in the military system that allowed unmanaged commanders to take advantage of soldiers to further their own careers and retirement packages. Kevin went to jail because those in command took full advantage of their rank to abuse the military justice system, believing there would be no retribution. Kevin was not like most soldiers these commanders chose to kick around. He was not going to quietly allow himself to be intimidated, and I was not going to let him face things alone. Someone had to put a stop to the injustices and abuse so many of our soldiers face.

Kevin and I continued to publicize conditions at the Fort Lewis RCF; we addressed the concerns of family members over the treatment of inmates there, and the mishandling of their individual legal cases. We wrote about the personal circumstances of many military families whose members had written to us asking for help. Many of these people contacted us after making several attempts to seek assistance from the national organizations prominently displaying their support of the troops and their families on their Web sites, posters, and banners, and at table displays for the various antiwar rallies they arranged, but getting no response to their requests for help.

It became increasingly clear—these organizations cared no more for the individual soldiers or their families than the administration that had sent us to war.

It was frustrating to watch those who professed to be activists for peace making every effort to be arrested by breaking laws meant to serve the common good, while my husband sat in a loss of privilege bay for daring to speak out against injustice, breaking no law in the process. If the activists were truly concerned about bringing justice and seeking truth, they did not need to invent ways to get themselves arrested to challenge laws. There were plenty of inmates in jail unjustly—wouldn't it have made more sense for these organizations to pick cases that had happened without any preconceived planning and publicize those? Wouldn't justice have been more appropriately served had these groups used their resources to address the needs of those who had quietly faced mistreatment and refused to violate their own principles regardless of how demanding the intimidation became? I knew that was not going to happen.

I was disappointed with those organizations that claimed to be for the troops, knowing in reality they were simply acting for themselves. Not all activists we encountered were caught up in the enjoyment of the notoriety their public protests brought, however. We have met wonderful individuals who did care, who wanted real change, and continue to work to see change happen. What we have come to know is that those who care about the real work, the right work, rarely receive the attention they deserve and never seek publicity for themselves.

An organization in the Seattle area contacted me and asked if it could do something to help Kevin's situation. The group wanted to hold some rallies outside the gates of Fort Lewis and publicize Kevin's name and story in the hope of making the soldiers at Fort Lewis and civilians in the area more aware of what was happening. Kevin and I talked about this. We were hesitant at first, not wanting to be drawn into the political games most organizations seemed to direct their attention toward. After many conversations with the organizers of this group project, it became clear they only wanted to do something to help Kevin, and they were willing to allow us to dictate how they were to proceed.

We asked that the events be strictly for conscientious objection, about Kevin's case, and the situation of any soldiers in similar circumstances. We asked that there be no mention of personal beliefs regarding the policy of the Iraq war, or personal sentiments directed at our administration. We wanted to generate a public discussion about positive alternatives and solutions to war. We did not want to divide our country further by taking a public stand with a personal vendetta. We had seen enough of that; we lived with soldiers who felt the ramifications of a divided nation, and we were not going to be party to adding fuel to the already incredibly hot fire the military personnel and their families faced. For us, the focus had to remain on the soldiers and the support they so desperately needed from civilians, from the administration, and from the policy makers who could ensure adequate changes were made to a disorganized and oftentimes corrupt military system.

We allowed the bannering events to proceed, but we were cautious. We paid attention to feedback and to the type of publicity the events drew. The division of soldiers stationed at Fort Lewis was due to deploy to Iraq in the coming months, and we did not want to distract attention from what they were about to face, even as we hoped to draw attention to the message Kevin wanted to send.

Toward the end of April, Kevin received word that the parole board had made its decision to deny his request for parole. The reasons cited were ridiculous and pointed directly to the concern the military continued to have over Kevin's calling public attention to the truth and to the lack of respect so many of those in command positions had for military regulations and U.S. law. The parole board said it was denying Kevin's request because he had "not been sufficiently rehabilitated" and "had not served enough of his sentence." We were not surprised. We moved forward, working on Kevin's appeal and on creating publicity for his case to show what not holding the military accountable to the rule of law could do to a soldier, the soldier's family, and their lives. Many soldiers whose names would never reach a public forum were facing the injustice of an uncontrolled military justice system.

I also was contacted by the caseworker from our congressional representative's office, which had received a letter from the director of the parole board in Virginia for the Department of the Army. The letter was dated April 23. It was a formal invitation to the members of the congressional office who wished to make a statement on Kevin's behalf for the parole board hearing. It also informed them that I, as his wife, would be given the same opportunity. I never received any word from the RCF or the parole board that I would be able to offer a personal statement to be added to Kevin's parole packet for consideration by the board. Unfortunately, the letter mailed to the congressional office was not received until almost one month after the board had made its decision to deny Kevin's request for parole. There was nothing we could do.

May 2006

Monica Kevin was released from the loss of privilege bay for what turned out to be only two weeks. It was not long before the publicity we were generating and the statements Kevin continued to make brought new concern to the command and staff at the RCF. One afternoon Kevin and the other inmates responded to a fire drill by moving outside and standing in formation to be accounted for. After members of the cadre had completed their count, the inmates were released to stay at ease in the yard outside the facility until it was clear they could return inside. Two members of the guard approached Kevin while he was sitting on a picnic table bench and ordered him to stand. When Kevin questioned their reason for singling him out from all the other inmates sitting in various locations in the yard, the guard members issued another discipline and adjustment report and filed it with the warden.

An inmate is not allowed to be represented by an attorney during a discipline and adjustment hearing, but the regulations entitle him to seek advice from his attorney prior to the board's convening. One day after Kevin was issued the report, the warden scheduled a one-man board hearing, denying Kevin his right to speak to an attorney before the hearing. Kevin called me late one afternoon to ask for help in handling this. I contacted everyone I knew who might be able to assist him. The caseworker from our congressional office made phone calls to the facility to speak to Kevin. We had been working on raising funds to retain a civilian attorney who could assist with Kevin's appeal, and we had spoken to one very well-respected attorney, himself a conscientious objector with a clear understanding of military law. He had connections with several antiwar and veterans' organizations as well.

We had not yet been able to raise the funds needed, but I called him anyway. He had already attempted to meet with Kevin at the RCF while handling another inmate's case. The meeting did not happen. Kevin was serving in loss of privilege at the time, and not being able to facilitate the paperwork process needed in time for the visit, nothing could be done about it. There was nothing this attorney could do either, and nothing he seemed willing to do without the guarantee of a retainer fee in hand.

I contacted the military Appellate Division in Virginia and spoke with the commanding officer. He was familiar with Kevin's case already as we had spoken several times since the convening authority had signed Kevin's record of trial, and he had been very helpful in advising us on the appeal process. This man was one individual in the military hierarchy that we came to develop a strong belief in. He is caring, considerate, and extremely knowledgeable, and it is clear that the welfare of the soldiers is important to him. When I notified him of the treatment Kevin was receiving at the RCF, he wasted no time in contacting the trial defense office at Fort Lewis and arranging for communication between one of their attorneys and Kevin. He also contacted the RCF directly and was able to have the hearing postponed until after Kevin spoke with an attorney. Finally, within the military, we had found someone with integrity who understood the regulations and sought to ensure they were followed.

Kevin was ultimately given an additional sixty days in the loss of privilege bay for not standing at attention. This sentence was generally reserved for those inmates involved in an assault or a similar infraction. Once again it was clear that the warden, the staff, and the command at the RCF were going to do whatever they could to lessen as much as possible the public attention Kevin drew to their facility in the time remaining on his sentence. We sensed they were simply shutting down as many lines of communication as they could to create less pressure on themselves; they were as anxious for Kevin's release date to arrive as we were.

Kevin and I do not expect anyone to do anything for free. Everyone has bills and a lifestyle to pay for, and we were grateful to those who did help us along the way, sacrificing some of their own income and time to do what they could to keep Kevin's message alive and his home intact while he was incarcerated. There were many individuals to thank for their support during this time. We would not think of disrespecting their gift of friendship and strength. They were quiet in their giving, asking only that we continue to move forward in our actions, continually reminding us that the work we did was as much for them as ourselves. We were always aware of that, and it was one reason we continue to carefully consider our actions, the possible consequences they might cause, and the influence they may have on others, before we take any real steps.

We were aware that many people and organizations would have liked to take advantage of the position Kevin and I had taken and the message we sought to convey by using our names to further their agenda. Many of these groups had already used our statements, manipulating them to reflect agreement with their own public positions, and they did so without our approval or concern for the effect it would have on Kevin's case, or our lives. We respect the fact that we chose to make Kevin's case public and therefore opened ourselves up to all manner of recognition, media attention, scrutiny, and criticism. It was our choice, and the manner in which it continued was our choice as well. There was nothing we could do except continue to work on the issues that mattered to us, and to personally represent our position as clearly as possible so that it would not be misconstrued or confused. What we hoped was that those who did understand and those who shared our perspective would come to see our actions as they were meant to be seen, and that our actions were in keeping with the trust their support showed. Good people—not organizations, not groups representing policy, but individuals, human beings—quietly gave us their trust, and we did not want to disrespect what they had given to us.

Kevin and I preferred to work publicly as a team; we *were* a team, after all. Throughout the time Kevin was serving his sentence, I had been asked to speak at several different events. Each time I would discuss it with Kevin first, and while it always seemed appropriate that I attend the events to speak and read a prepared statement from Kevin, it wasn't the same as attending the events together. We had done so several times in the months leading up to his courts-martial and not only enjoyed the work together, but also felt that the message was far more effective when we shared the words. So I had not participated in any public events without Kevin while he was incarcerated.

Toward the end of April I received an e-mail from the caseworker at our representative's office where the staff was working on hosting a special congressional briefing on conscientious objection, to be presented during International Conscientious Objectors' Day on May 15. They had hoped that Kevin's parole would go through and Kevin and I would be able to attend the briefing together, but that did not happen. They wanted me to attend regardless and make a statement about Kevin's case and our position on conscientious objection. Again I spoke with Kevin. This time the event seemed different from an antiwar rally where my words could easily be lost in the rally's public demand for attention. This briefing was to be a representation of conscientious objection, educational in nature, and an opportunity to present Kevin's case to an audience that should have been hearing more of what our individual soldiers were facing for living by their principles, freely choosing a moral position against war and speaking publicly about it.

It was difficult to make the trip to Washington, DC, without Kevin, but it was well worth it. I was able to meet people we had communicated with by e-mail and letters for the past two years and thank them for their advice and support. I was able to express our position face-to-face and discuss particulars of Kevin's case with many people who were not aware of the difficulties he continued to have simply for speaking the truth in public.

While in Washington, I took time to visit the memorials on the National Mall and stopped to watch the activities of antiwar organizations mobilized for protests in front of the Washington Monument. I did not participate in the rallies or events. I understood the reasons people felt the need to do what they did, and just as Kevin and I were asking to be given respect for making our personal choices, I had to allow them the same respect in return. As I watched the people participating and those walking by, observing, I did my best to try to understand why these activities continued. From my perspective, just as Kevin has been saying, war should be obsolete. I felt public protests should be heading in that direction as well.

The destructive force of war was the greatest violation of peace imaginable, and yet some of those who spoke out against war seemed to be violating peace in a different sense. I think it is good for people to learn from different perspectives, but I do not believe we have the right to decide when and how that happens, except for ourselves, and I felt that the public protests were geared toward demanding rather than teaching new perspectives. I believe the information can be presented in a mature, respectful manner, and those who are ready will ask the questions. Those who are not have the right to choose not to listen and to have that right respected.

I did not feel comfortable with the protest marches and massive antiwar rallies, especially in public arenas meant for the enjoyment of all people. I never was one to come to another's way of thinking if someone shouted at me. I think, to some degree, my discomfort came not only from how the issues were being presented but also from the personal attacks that seemed to go hand in hand with the protests. I did my best to reconcile in my own mind the reasons and the need for the conflict between war and peace. It was personal, and others were entitled to their own thoughts.

The protesters seemed to believe their public displays were justified by the Constitution's allowance of freedom of speech and the right to peaceably assemble. I couldn't find room to question freedom of speech, but I had my doubts about their interpretation of peaceable assembly and nonviolence. A federal law requiring permits for public events was continuously questioned by protesters. I couldn't see the reason for this. I understood the rights of those making public statements, but I also understood the need for obtaining a permit to protect the rights of those who did not want to hear the public statements. On a personal level, I was more than willing to allow people the right to say what they had to say, but I expected them to respect my right to privacy as well. In the protests I witnessed, I saw freedom of speech being demonstrated, but I was lost when it came to finding respect for the right to privacy for those who did not want to listen.

Our beliefs about war are widely known, and Kevin and I have spoken at several events organized against war. People are invited to attend, and they are given the opportunity to decide for themselves if the theme of each event is something they want to hear. Permits are granted and public notice of the event is given in advance so those who do not wish to participate know to stay away. These events were done with respect for all and allowed people the freedom to make their own decisions peacefully. Setting up information tables at functions that allowed all sides to present their position made sense to me, in the spirit of our Constitution and our right to freedom of choice. Shouting into bullhorns and microphones on a public mall, regardless of the position being taken, sounded more like children throwing temper tantrums than anything else. If they couldn't get their way, they would yell loudly until someone acted, simply to get them to stop yelling. People will come to things in their own time, and they may not ever reach the position others believe they should. But it is their right to choose their position. If the information about war vividly shown on television screens and newspapers every night is not enough to make people come to their senses about war, the consequences of their choices are theirs. We can provide information in many forms, but it is up to individuals to learn their own lessons.

As I walked around our National Mall, I stopped at the reflecting pool and realized that no matter how far down the pathway I walked, I could still hear the assembled protesters demanding that their rights be respected. The National Mall is rich in history, with monuments from one end to the other, representing memorials to veterans of every war ever fought by Americans. People from all over the world travel to Washington to stand and pay their respects to those who died in service to our country. I realize that many believed they were serving to defend the freedoms our Constitution granted all citizens, but I continue to believe public protests in a place of honor for the history of our country is inappropriate, especially when the protests reflect the personal attacks we continue to see. It is hard to trust the words of people who are willing to lower their standards to the same level as those they are criticizing. If we must stand at a microphone and shout demands for people to come to our way of thinking, then it doesn't seem that our way of thinking is all that we believe it to be. My peace was violated by the Iraq war, and yet with every national protest I witnessed, I felt my peace was also violated by those loudest proponents of peace.

Soldiers stationed at Fort Lewis were preparing to deploy to Iraq for their second tour. We had heard from a few military personnel from Fort Lewis via e-mail. They had learned of Kevin's case through the bannering events held every month on a bridge near one of the gates of the installation. We were proud of the way these bannering events had happened. We felt they had been handled with respect for opposing views, and in a manner that protected the rights of those who chose a different view.

The bridge had first been used by a group of military families who strongly supported the soldiers and left yellow ribbons and patriotic flowers hanging across the walkways to remind those passing under and over that our country was at war and soldiers were serving. During one of the weekend events a bit of verbal conflict erupted between two groups on the bridge. Those who had been handing out information about Kevin's case felt they would be better off moving to a different location. We asked them not to. We believed what was happening on the bridge was exactly what Kevin and I hoped to pursue with others. Both sides of the divided country were being represented together in one place, and it was important for people to see it happening and participate in it. We hoped that members of both sides would learn a little more about each other, and that the door to understanding open just a little wider along the way. We also hoped that the discussions would help each side to realize the need to address soldiers' rights as citizens and as the first-line defenders of those rights, and perhaps come to find a common ground to work together to ensure those rights, regardless of their feelings about this war.

We heard from many of the participants that cars stopped on the way to the gate and occupants asked for information that was being distributed. Many were not interested in what was being handed out, and it was not offered to them. Some soldiers came from the installation in uniform to speak to those bannering and asked to learn more. They were looking for more information about conscientious objection. Those who contacted us directly from our handouts were directed to resources that might help them with their personal decisions. We felt the events had been handled respectfully. Some of the guards at the RCF had come to understand and accept Kevin's actions and position. They quietly supported him and asked questions of him as well. Several reported the bannering events to Kevin, and a few of the guards stopped to talk to those bannering to assure them they knew

Kevin, would tell him about the event, and to let the people know that Kevin was a good man.

We had also learned that some activist groups in the Seattle area were encouraging soldiers to run from deployment, even going so far as to offer sanctuary in a local church to avoid deploying. It is against the law to knowingly encourage a member of the military to desert, and the penalty is much stiffer during a time of war. Soldiers volunteer to defend our laws. It angered me that those who claimed to be supporting the soldiers were encouraging them to break the law in an effort to gain enough resistance to influence an end to the war.

Kevin and I could not condone this. We were contacted by members of these organizations to ask if we would join in encouraging soldiers to resist orders to deploy; we would not. Regulations are in place to allow soldiers to leave the service in a legal manner. If soldiers can no longer serve in war, if their conscience will no longer allow them to be part of what they had volunteered to do, regulations allow them the right to say no. When soldiers run from their service, when they are not willing to stand up for what they believe, it does nothing except weaken their position.

We heard from activists asking us to give our support to those who had deserted to Canada rather than return to war. We would not. Running simply created a new set of consequences, and until those who had deserted were willing to stand up and face the consequences, they were always going to be on the run. Even if the day comes when some future president offers amnesty for those who deserted, the fact is, they will always have the stigma of being a deserter to carry with them. If they believe strongly enough that what the military has been asked to do is wrong, the best way to ensure that we can stop it is to stand boldly against it, not hide and challenge it from darkened corners. Kevin believed in his position against war enough that he was willing to face the consequences from the army, even as it used deceptive practices to convict him. The fact that his conviction required deceptive practices simply confirmed his position even more strongly. Why would you run from the truth if you truly believed in it as the truth?

Peace advocates wanted the war ended, but they did not seem to care what position they put the soldiers in to get it done. We had heard from many Vietnam veterans since the beginning of the public madness we faced; so many had deserted, run away rather than make a public, legal stand of opposition to the war. So many veterans had told us how much they wished they had not run but had stood firmly and publicly as Kevin had, defending their right to conscience and forcing the military to abide by its own regulations. If they had done so, the power of their statements together could have brought about a far more significant change, and it is a change we hope to work together for now. People want the truth, and it's hard to trust the words of those who have chosen to run rather than face head-on what they know to be wrong. Truth is strong. Truth is powerful without any complexity. Truth is simple. If we are speaking the truth, what reason do we have to hide in a church sanctuary? If we are speaking the truth, why would we not speak it boldly, proudly, and in the bright light where others who feel as we do will hear and join us? Why would we run?

As the time approached for the Fort Lewis units to deploy, we asked those who had been doing the banner events on Kevin's behalf to stop. We had been through deployments and knew the emotional turmoil they created. The situation in Iraq had become far worse over the three years we had been at war, and it would not have been appropriate for us to interfere with the ordeal the Fort Lewis soldiers and their families were facing with the impending deployment. Kevin's position was widely known, and his case had drawn international attention. We appreciated the effort everyone had made in helping to see that the military was aware that the public was witnessing their actions against Kevin. Nonetheless, we were not going to disrespect those soldiers who continued to serve.

I believe that people on both sides of this war need to stop and consider the opposing perspectives. Throughout the three years we were involved on both sides of the conflict, we saw how little the opposite sides were willing to listen to what made each believe their position was right. Those who strongly supported the military actions did so believing it was the best way to achieve peace. Those who strongly opposed those same military actions did so believing they also were moving in the best direction for achieving peace. Neither side ever seemed to stop to consider the possibility of reaching a common understanding and moving forward with a dialogue that would lead us all to a real peace, undivided. Even more, neither side made any real effort to see how little their debates did for the military personnel and their families. As opposing parties became more intent on pursuing their own agendas, the needs of the military personnel were being forgotten. Policy became more important than humanity, again.

June and July 2006

Monica There was little more we could do from a legal standpoint in Kevin's case except ride out the balance of his sentence and wait for the date to file his appeal. At first we continued to seek assistance getting funds for a civilian attorney, and we appreciated the donations we received that helped defray our living expenses as well. We continued to speak with civilian attorneys and advocates about Kevin's case, but we were frustrated by the fact that they all wanted to handle Kevin's appeal with a discussion of the illegality of the war, using his case to create a public prosecution of the administration.

Kevin and I had considered all of that prior to his filing his conscientious objector application. Regardless of our personal feelings about the Iraq war, they were personal feelings not meant to be presented in a public display of judgment against the war. We knew what we had learned, and Kevin most assuredly knew what he had experienced, but they were *our* experiences. We did not have all the facts, and we were not party to all the policy decisions made by administration officials and Congress. A military court-martial is not the place to argue the illegality of a war. Soldiers, once having taken their oath of service, are no longer citizens who participate in policy making or in judging the legality of the actions of the administration. Soldiers are defenders of policy, and in their position, their actions are based on trusting the leadership to commit their service only to legal policy. The military justice system is not set up to allow military personnel to question policy. They do have a right to question illegal orders, however, when given by the command in specific instances of combat and training. They do have a right to conscientiously object to war on the basis of changed beliefs crystallizing after their initial oath is taken.

In Kevin's case, he filed a conscientious objector application as his legal refusal to further participate in war. What we couldn't seem to get any civilian attorney to understand was that his application was never given due process and that the basis of his appeal was not his belief in the illegality of the war, but the command's inability to produce any evidence that he had refused an order to deploy, manipulating testimony and documents to give the impression that evidence existed when it clearly did not.

Ultimately Kevin decided not to retain civilian counsel for the appeal of his court-martial verdict. After continued conversations with his appointed military appellate counsel and that attorney's superiors, it became clear that they understood Kevin's defense and the reasons we believed Kevin had been unjustly convicted. Throughout the courts-martial the prosecution covered its tracks and filed motions expecting Kevin to use the illegality of the war as a defense. It set up as many roadblocks to that defense as possible, but that was never needed. Even knowing Kevin's and my personal feelings about the Iraq war, and knowing we had sought advice on how to resolve those feelings in a legal manner, they did not ever come into play in Kevin's duty to the army. His command violated regulations and in its incompetence sought to cover its mistakes by bringing charges against Kevin. The incompetence showed itself repeatedly in the army's prosecution of Kevin's courts-martial, from the convening authority on down to the rear detachment commander, and yet Kevin went to jail because no one had the integrity to step in and hold the command accountable to regulations.

When we asked civilians in legal positions to help, everyone wanted to look past the simple defense in Kevin's appeal, which was holding the command accountable for its lies, manipulations, and deceit, turning instead to using Kevin's case as a sacrifice to speak out against the administration. No one was able to see the humanity of this soldier and the simple need to defend his right to conscience against a corrupt command. This inability on the part of the civilian sector to understand our situation is something we hope to overcome. Life is far simpler than many people want to believe it can be. I believe we must start looking to simple solutions and simple understanding, communicating on the most basic levels, reaching out for commonality while not forgetting our differences. People have lost sight of the simple aspects of being human, coming to believe that everything must be analyzed in the most complex manner possible to reach any answers.

As far as Kevin's case is concerned, he followed regulations every step of the way and tried from the start to find one member of his chain of command who was willing to do the same in regard to his conscientious objector application. Not only was the command unwilling, it was also incompetent and ignorant of the regulations it claimed to have followed. Every step of the way the command was playing catch-up to its own inability to play by the rules, and Kevin paid the price for his command's inadequate leadership. The simple message in all of this is that a soldier has the right to live by his conscience, and if he follows regulations, he is entitled to expect his commanders to do the same.

Kevin stood by the truth, and his command could not respond in kind. This is the basic injustice Kevin faced. Finally, a captain in the military Appellate Division was able to see the picture clearly. We had come full circle. A captain serving as Kevin's company commander, in total disregard for the regulations he was sworn to uphold, used every means possible to punish Kevin for his strength of conviction. Kevin was now placing his trust in another army captain who clearly saw the injustice in how Kevin's courts-martial were conducted. Kevin was still in prison, but we were one step closer to returning to our own longed-for peace.

August 2006

Monica The time for Kevin's release was drawing close. He had completed serving his time in the loss of privilege bay, and his good behavior time meant he would be released almost six weeks before his full sentence was served. This was good. We were both ready for the madness to be done. Nothing that had happened during the past three and a half years had made much sense. We had lived through some interesting times and faced a great number of challenges. It was hard to believe all the experiences we had managed to face in such a short time together. Lifetimes had happened, and we were just beginning.

We went through many different emotions in the time remaining. We had many good friends in the Seattle area and wanted to be able to thank them all for everything they had done for us during the last year, but at the same time we wanted to move on quietly from the madness. We thought about arranging a picnic to meet with a few of the most significant people involved in publicizing support for Kevin. We wanted to do something special. We also considered everything we had been through and knew in the end there would be plenty of time for thanking people. First, we needed some time for ourselves. We had come to feel very strongly about many of the people in the Seattle area. They had done so much for us and seemed to understand our position and relationship more than most. They listened and worked with us as far as publicity and privacy were concerned. We hoped they would understand if we took a little time for ourselves before we gave to others.

We had hoped to be able to arrange my moving to the Seattle area before Kevin was released from the RCF, but it did not happen. Now we know it was for the best. Home was here and it was what Kevin knew. When he first left for Fort Lewis, a year seemed like such a long time, and I wanted to be as close as I could to the facility he was confined in so that I could visit him as often as I was allowed. The first reaction was to move immediately, and I began to make plans to do so. In retrospect, it was an expected reaction, and it was encouraged by many of the people who supported us. I heard what they were saying and allowed myself to be influenced without thinking things through. After Kevin went to prison in Seattle, and we adjusted somewhat to the new life we had been forced into, I realized it was temporary. I also remembered that we worked best as a team. We needed to be together to decide the next place, the next journey, and the next experience. Most of all, Kevin needed to have the memories of this place, our present home. Just as he had needed to have memories while he was in Iraq, it was important that we could talk about places familiar to him, and he would know that familiarity would be there when he was released.

Kevin went through quite an ordeal. The army wanted to make sure he paid the greatest price it could extract for his daring to stand against the policy of war and for his own evolving values and principles for life. The army made things as difficult as possible every step of the way. There are many experiences that I know he will never talk about, but I don't need to hear them. I knew from my own firsthand experiences with a mismanaged, corrupt command the extent to which it was willing to go to attempt to intimidate a soldier who stood against it and refused to break. It was important for home to be what

Kevin remembered so he could return to it and find some peace after the past year of total chaos.

August 18, 2006

Monica Kevin was released. We told four people. The groups in Seattle had been gracious. We look forward to having that picnic with them all one day soon.

Kevin called in the morning to let me know he was free and at the Seattle airport. A good friend in Atlanta had arranged the flights Kevin took. He is another one we are grateful to, and we hope he knows just how much we appreciate what he did for us.

The day went by more quickly than I thought it would. Before long it was evening and time to head to the airport to wait a little longer. The Savannah airport is small and quiet. I sat in a rocking chair with my son sitting nearby and waited. It was a good feeling, and knowing that we had been successful in keeping the news of Kevin's release a veritable secret made it all just a little more special. We are willing to share our experiences with as many people around the world who wanted to hear them, but that night, it was nice to know that there was no one in the world who had a part in what we were living except the two of us, three kids, and a very few good friends. There would be plenty of time for publicity. We had plans. We will see them through. Veterans and active-duty military chose a challenging direction. It is time a real effort is made to give them the respect they have earned with more than yellow ribbons, memorial parades, and lip service on the congressional house floors and in antiwar protest marches.

When Kevin came through the gate, we saw that he had put on a little weight and grown a mustache, but we had no trouble recognizing him. Once again I was reminded of the circles life makes and had a strong sense of déjà vu as shades of Iraq, the deployment, the past year he had spent in prison, and now his coming home all tangled together as I sat in the airport staring at a giant pendulum clock swaying slowly from the dome in the center of the ceiling; the time that had stopped for so long seemed to finally be ready to start again. Everything was strangely familiar, and I was grateful thinking that some things do not change, even in war.

Kevin was home again. We were where we needed to be, and in time we would make plans for the next adventure on our journey together. First we would spend some quiet time together, repairing the cracks in the foundation caused by military commanders who had no sense of humanity. Next we would set new goals, create a new plan, and move forward. No matter what, we would move forward. There really is no other way.

War has the potential to change everything. There are some things stronger than war.

6: Letters from a Fort Lewis Brig

Monica During the months leading to Kevin's courts-martial, we had been contacted by thousands of people who supported his stand. It was interesting how closely attached some had become to our story. At one point, we made some minor cosmetic changes to our Web site. The next day, we received an e-mail from a loyal supporter who was quite upset at the changes. She wrote that she was used to having her morning coffee while reading the new postings on our site and the changes had disturbed her comfort zone. The connections clearly mattered. We changed the Web site back.

The week after Kevin was taken to the prison at Fort Lewis, many of our supporters began asking about him and how to contact him. Knowing this was going to be impossible, we elected for Kevin to prepare a statement that we would post on the Web site to assure people that he was okay. It was doubtful that the prison officials would have allowed such a statement to leave the facility through the mail; there were innumerable stories of censorship from that prison. Kevin decided to read the statement to me during one of his phone calls. I copied the words down and then typed them for the Web site.

The response to Kevin's statement was overwhelming, and it wasn't long before people were calling to hear from him again. I bought a cassette recorder and plenty of tapes. Once a week, Kevin would gather his thoughts into a new statement, read them to me over the phone, and I would transcribe the taped words for posting on the Web site.

Spring arrived and prison officials seemed frustrated over Kevin's ability to continue communicating with the outside world. They found trivial reasons to keep him in their loss of privilege bay for months at a time, hoping to keep him quiet, so there were no postings for several months. After a time, he once again found a way to get to a phone and read his statements to me for posting, and his "Letters from a Fort Lewis Brig" resumed. Here they are, from the beginning of his incarceration to the time of his release:

August 12, 2005

I have immense respect for all the veterans, and now the Vietnam veterans, the Gulf War veterans, and those returning from Iraq with me. These veterans that have put their lives on the line for their country deserve all of the honor we can give them.

One of the chief reasons for the stand that I am taking is to show that respect for these veterans, and to see that others who don't understand, also come to respect our sacrifice. Our soldiers and veterans are human beings first—I can attest to that with my own life—and we all deserve to be treated as human beings first and then as soldiers who have given what we can to defend our country through our service. Agent Orange, Depleted Uranium, mistreated PTSD, disrupted families, and a country that will not make a concerted effort to work toward alternative solutions to war are blatant signs of disrespect for our service.

I stand to honor those who fought in wars to see that wars would end. I laid down my gun so that my life will represent my words honestly. I believe there is a better way than war, and I stand to honor those soldiers who have come to know that the last thing they want to have to do is go to war. Defense of our country should not get to the extreme of war.

We should do all that we can to honor the service of our veterans, to make changes in our policies that allow us to remain safe and protected from those who would want to disrupt our peace, so that we can avert our need for war, and teach our children a better way.

Sgt. Kevin Benderman,
Conscientious Objector to War

August 17, 2005
On August 5, 2005, kind and brave people in Iraq held prayers for me in over 100 mosques throughout their country as a show of human kindness to me because of my decision to no longer take part in war. It amazes me that despite everything they're dealing with, they took the time to consider my actions and show human kindness and support for me. I am honored by this display of compassion.

This is how the common citizens of any country can rid humanity of the scourge of wars, by laying down their weapons and extending their hand to their fellow brothers and sisters.

Politics cannot end wars, but people can. So, why don't we combine our efforts worldwide to put an end to the senselessness of war?

Sgt. Kevin Benderman,
Conscientious Objector to War

August 25, 2005
There comes a time in a person's life when they have to reexamine the course they have set for themselves to see if it's best for them to continue. I was a U.S. soldier for ten years of my life, and after I had experienced war firsthand, I came to a personal crossroad.

The decision for me was rather complex, as there were many factors that had a bearing on my course of action. One was the fact that there had been a member of the military in my family since the American Revolution. Also, the area where I was raised has a strong sense of the military as being one of the most honorable things you can do. Being a soldier in the service of your country is a proud tradition for many American families; it cannot be denied, and it is most definitely not to be discouraged.

But isn't it time we reconsidered war as a way to settle differences among nations? When are we going to realize that creating and using weapons that are capable of killing scores of people in a single blow is a rather barbaric and outmoded way in which to solve our differences? If as much effort were put into solving our differences with positive resolutions as the world has put into developing weapons that are able to wipe out entire countries at a time, war could have been eradicated decades ago, as were various other diseases that we have worked to eliminate. Make no mistake; war is a disease that threatens all of humanity. Isn't it time to dedicate energy, efforts, and resources to eliminate this scourge of mankind? I believe it is.

I have laid down my weapons of war to pick them up never again. It is my sincere hope that more people will do the same so that our children and grandchildren will never have to experience what so many of us already have—the single most barbaric of human endeavors, otherwise known as war.

Sgt. Kevin Benderman,
Conscientious Objector to War

August 26, 2005

I have been observing this event at President Bush's ranch in Texas unfold, and I feel it is growing into something far beyond what you would expect from people who claim to be demanding respect for the Americans that have died in this war.

On the one hand there is a group of people looking for a peaceful solution, led by a mother whose son has died while in service to America. On the other hand there is a group telling them they are anti-American because they would like to see this war end and have no more people die.

What I believe both sides have lost sight of is that our young men and women who wear the uniform are dying in war; many civilians in Iraq have died as well because of war. Now the "opposing sides" at home are going to enter a shouting-down match to prove which side is "right."

How much more disrespectful can you get?

There was one man who decided to run over the crosses that held the names of our soldiers, marines, and other service members who have died, just so he could "show them," the people seeking a peaceful solution, that he was more American than they were.

The people who have died as a result of this failed policy of war, and I mean all war, deserve to be treated with much more dignity and respect than was shown by his actions. We need to focus our energies on permanently resolving the problems that are the root causes of war, because war is the destroyer of everything that is good about our world. It solves nothing, as evidenced by the fact that we are still fighting wars in this day and age. I want to quote someone who helped drop the bomb on Hiroshima, Japan: "The whole World War II experience shows that wars don't settle anything and atomic weapons don't settle anything. I personally think there shouldn't be any atomic weapons in the world. I would like to see them all abolished" (Theodore Van Kirk, navigator of the *Enola Gay*).

If we are supposed to learn from the people that have gone before us, then we are required to listen to them. Those are some rather powerful words which I believe we should all heed.

Sgt. Kevin Benderman,
Conscientious Objector to War

September 2, 2005
"I will not compromise my integrity, nor my moral courage."

These words come directly from the NCO creed, which I swore to uphold as a member of the U.S. Army. When I filed for conscientious objector status, it was after careful consideration of my duty to my wife, my stepchildren, my country, and the soldiers I served with. But before I could consider all of this, I had to consider myself. I had to ensure that my actions did not compromise what I believed in and what I stood for. I had served in Iraq, and I had seen the destruction war brings. After careful thought, I knew that I did not believe in war as an answer, and I would not participate in it any longer.

People told me that I abandoned soldiers. I did not. I chose to no longer fight in wars, because wars will never save lives, and they will never bring about the changes we need to make. I stand for soldiers, with the hope their lives and service will be given the respect they deserve. People told me that I was a coward. They can believe that, but I know what it takes to stand on my principles against the tide, with the only certainty being that my wife stood with me. People told me that I was letting my country down. I disagree. I am standing to defend what our Constitution was founded on—moral principles.

We are learning hard lessons this week. The devastation brought by Hurricane Katrina is teaching us something important. As a country, we cannot take care of others until we have taken care of ourselves. As a soldier, to continue to participate in war would have violated my own principles. I would have destroyed myself and others if I had not chosen to maintain *my* integrity as my first consideration. To continue on the destructive path of war would have made me unable to help anyone to grow in positive ways, because I was not growing in positive ways.

I believe that we, as a country, need to return to our Constitution, the foundation of America. This country has compromised its integrity and lost its moral courage. We can't help others until we have fixed ourselves.

Sgt. Kevin Benderman,
Conscientious Objector to War

September 8, 2005

I am currently reading a book by a Vietnam veteran named William Broyles Jr., and in it he describes his evolution from a person that fought in the war as a soldier to one that wanted to see the humanity of his adversaries, so that he would be able to reclaim this very humanity for himself. I believe he did that, and in the process was able to see that the people he fought against were just as human as he, and not the savage, backward, subhuman creatures they were made out to be.

In the book, he tells of a man named Norman Morrison, who, on November 9, 1965, went to the Pentagon with his daughter, Emily, to protest the madness that war is. His protest was much more than carrying a sign or writing letters to his congressman. Norman Morrison, a Quaker, was so disgusted at the stupidity of war that he doused himself with gasoline and burned himself to death.

I will close this with a quote from George Bernard Shaw: "The worst sin towards our fellow creatures has not been to hate them, but to be indifferent to them. That's the essence of inhumanity."

Sgt. Kevin Benderman,
Conscientious Objector to War

September 16, 2005

"Am I therefore become your enemy because I tell you the truth?"

It is an interesting question, and a thought-provoking one, from the Bible. It is one that, I believe, is the essence of why I am in jail. The truth I told grew from my experiences in the war in Iraq. I went there with the desire to avenge the people who died on September 11, 2001, and to keep the soldiers that I served with safe in the process. I went as a soldier in the service of my country, never once thinking that my government would mislead me or lie to me, not in order to advance the good of the country but to fulfill a seemingly personal agenda of a few individuals. The truth that I had to tell came from meeting the people that I had been told were bloodthirsty religious fanatics who were intent on destroying my country and our way of life, and discovering that aside from a few zealots, the assertion was just not the truth.

Zealotry is a very prominent, driving force in the world, and all countries, peoples, and religions have them [zealots]. Yes, there are zealots even within our highly esteemed Christianity, as evidenced by Pat Robertson calling for our government to assassinate the elected president of Venezuela. My pointing out fanaticism from within our own government, and the lies told in order to start the slaughter of a nation that had nothing to do with the September 11 attack on our country, is why I was taken before a kangaroo court and imprisoned as a result. The garrison commander told the prosecutors that I was to do eighteen months in prison before the investigation phase of the court-martial even started. The company commander was trying to come up with everything he could think of to smear me before they concentrated their efforts to put me in jail.

I do not want to mislead anyone into thinking that I am a saint, because I have done many things in my life that are wrong and I am ashamed of doing them. But, I decided that I was not going to add to that list by taking any further part in this war against a people that have done absolutely nothing to us.

Tacitus, a Roman historian, said, "When monarchs through their bloodthirsty commanders lay waste a country, they dignify their atrocity by calling it 'making peace,'" or in this case, by calling it "spreading democracy."

Sgt. Kevin Benderman,
Conscientious Objector to War

September 19, 2005

I have made a decision to choose what I want to do with my life, and it seems to have created a large controversy among people that are thoroughly entrenched within their own state of mind. My decision was one of a personal nature and has stirred up the proverbial hornet's nest on either side of the subject.

You see, my decision was to no longer participate in war after having experienced its insanity firsthand during Operation Iraqi Freedom. After growing up in a climate that glorifies war, being inundated with movies and other media that want to sanitize war, I went to the war in Iraq, and I realized that the entire business is so basically obscene and utterly inhuman, that I wanted nothing else to do with it. People reacted violently to my decision. I was labeled a "coward," and even had my patriotism brought into question.

This led me to ask, "Are we so entrenched in the love of war in America that we cannot begin to see how to start moving away from it as a source of national identity and pride?"

If I kill someone with a high-powered assault rifle, why does that make me a better citizen?

I believe we are long overdue for placing as much effort into developing more positive solutions to disagreements as we do on maintaining a force for destruction. As mature, intelligent people, we all have a choice, and I have made mine based on my personal experiences. Isn't that a fundamental right that we all have?

If so, why then was I placed in prison for making my choice? Don't get me wrong; I was prepared to face the consequences of my actions, and I still am. But isn't it odd that I was put in prison for exercising the right guaranteed me by the U.S. Constitution?

My conscience will no longer allow me to kill another human being in a war, nor will it allow me to assist anyone else to do so either. It is a sad day when that makes me less of an American than someone who chooses to participate in war. We must not condemn anyone who makes their own choice, but it is inherently unfair to those individuals, like me, to withhold pertinent information that is needed for them to make the best possible choice.

When I saw for myself what I was not shown before I went to war, I made my choice. In America, we are all free to make our choices. As an American soldier, that is what I stood for when I deployed to Iraq. As an American soldier, that is what I stand for now, having seen the horrors of war firsthand. I made my choice and continue to defend our Constitution in the process.

Last week, a woman was put to death in Texas because the courts said that she had killed her family.

I made the choice to no longer participate in war, the greatest open act of killing, and today I am in prison. Why?

Sgt. Kevin Benderman,
Conscientious Objector to War

September 21, 2005

Today, I would like to consider all the people who have died as a result of war. I would like to consider all the people who have been physically scarred as a result of war. I would like to consider all the people who are suffering mental and emotional trauma as a result of the ravages of war.

I want you to recall the pictures of the little girl running along the roadway in Vietnam, horribly burned from *our* use of napalm in that war.

And—I want to convey to you the image that I have of a young girl whose arm was burned terribly, and who was left standing by the side of the road, to fend for herself, because *our* fighting a war was more important than helping an injured child.

I want you to think of lives disrupted because of war. I want you to understand not seeing a child take his or her first steps, and their mom or dad missing that moment because of war. I want you to think of graduations, birthdays, anniversaries, weddings, births, and everything that makes up our lives, stolen from us as a result of being in a war.

I want you to think of the great men and women who will be forever missing from someone's life because of the stupidity and inhumanity of war. No one should have to suffer the anguish of burying a child, a brother, a sister, a mom, a dad, an aunt, an uncle, a husband, or wife because of war.

I want you to understand my father's horror at the atrocities of war he faced in WWII, and his struggle with incomprehension at my not grasping what he was trying to tell me about war.

I want you to think about why a veteran can be homeless and can lose benefits promised to him or her for having fought to defend this country in war.

But most of all, I want you to think about why we are even pursuing such an outmoded and barbaric institution as war to express our civilized desire to better the world in which we live.

Sgt. Kevin Benderman,
Conscientious Objector to War

September 29, 2005

Regional religious preferences have caused as much bloodshed as any of the other myriad justifications mankind has used to kill one another. One religious philosophy is persecuted by another, that is then persecuted by another, and so on. All this persecution of one group by another needs to stop because it goes against the basic idea of the law, which is to "love your neighbor as you do yourself."

So many people are caught up in the petty belief that the Creator recognizes only "them" as the chosen people. When are we going to realize that we are attempting the impossible by trying to fit the Creator of all life into an image that suits only us?

Do you not think that the power that created the entire universe, and all that it holds, has the ability to reach each person in a way that he or she understands?

That personal communication doesn't mean that we have exclusive rights to force others to adapt to our understanding. The Creator will interact with each people in a manner that works best for them to receive. It is not up to us to force anyone else to adopt what works for us.

Humanity should open its collective eyes and take a good, hard look at the mistakes we have made and will continue to make unless we admit to the fact that every one of us are alike and have the same basic needs. We speak different languages; we are peoples of many tongues. The Creator will come to us in the language and the books that each of understands, but the Creator comes to give us all the same things.

There is not one group of people that is superior to another. Humanity as a whole would be much better off if we could stop believing that one specific group is the "chosen one" and realize that we are all children of the Creator. Our efforts would be better spent assisting each other instead of killing each other over differences in how we worship the Creator.

It would benefit us all to put an end to all the meaningless reasons we conjure up in an attempt to justify our disruptive tendencies. How can we claim to have the Creator on our side in a war that was started by man's ideology, greed, or just plain human meanness? In all of the different tenets of religion that I have read, I have found the same basic philosophy:

"Thou shall not kill."

There are no qualifiers in that definitive statement. There are no disclaimers, excuses, or legal authority giving any of us the license to kill. It is simple and direct. "You shall not kill." The Creator wants all of humanity to live together peacefully. Isn't it time to start trying? Or—are we going to continue to lay the responsibility for our failures at the Creator's feet?

Sgt. Kevin Benderman,
Conscientious Objector to War

October 6, 2005
There are people who do not understand how someone can grow, develop, and change their perspective about things that they have been a part of for years. That is why some people seem to be having such a

hard time understanding why I, a soldier with ten years of honorable service, have now reached a new understanding about the futility and stupidity of war.

For many years I was influenced by and taught to admire war through the knowledge of a family history of military service, the regional influence of living in the South with Civil War memorials everywhere, and the basic teachings of our country's involvement in war throughout its history.

People who wanted to bring about change for the better through peaceful means were denigrated as un-American and unpatriotic. This makes me ask, "Why do you have to love the indiscriminate and destructive force of war to be considered a patriot???"

I do understand that there are some people who are against anything that concerned people in this country try to do that is a step away from the way we have always done things, and that is their right. But, if they do not like what is happening, then no one is keeping them here against their will. Peaceful resolutions will work, and there is progress toward making them a reality. But we must not lose sight of this progress, and we should not back down from our principles when those who do not see reason in a new way try to discourage us through fear.

I have a problem with Americans who want to continue to solve our problems with violence. We pay lip service to people like Mother Teresa, Martin Luther King Jr., and various others who have taught and continue to teach that our country would be better served through peaceful actions; all the while we are spending billions on developing more effective killing methods.

I have come to the conclusion that you can hate the violence and stupidity of war, yet love the country in which you were born and raised. War should not be a source of national identity and pride. To quote H. Norman Schwarzkopf, at the time a battalion commander in Vietnam: "War is a profanity, it really is. It is terrifying. Nobody is more antiwar than an intelligent person who has been to war."

That about sums it up.

Sgt. Kevin Benderman,
Conscientious Objector to War

October 13, 2005

It has been said that you should never question what the heads of government tell you is right, but I say that by the very way that the Constitution of this country is laid out, there is an expectation of every citizen to do just that.

It is every citizen's responsibility, as well as their inherent right, to question the motives of our elected leaders. Our form of government is unique in the world in that respect. Slowly we have allowed those that we have hired to serve us in our government to twist the intent of the founding fathers into what we now have. They now want us to believe that we are never supposed to question their actions or hold them accountable for the mistakes they make. And yet, in certain cases, there are actions they take which are blatantly illegal.

I believe it is past time for the citizens of this country to stand up and tell the people we have hired to work for us that we expect them to perform to the higher standard we have set for them.

It is time to let our employees know that we will not tolerate condescension from them. If they break the laws of this country, then they will be held accountable for what they are responsible for. They should not be able to pass the buck on their own insubordination to the American citizens for whom they work.

Sgt. Kevin Benderman,
Conscientious Objector to War

October 17, 2005

I would like to focus on the families of veterans of war, and what they have experienced as a result of loving someone who has to go to war. The wives, sons, daughters, and more recently, the husbands of war fighters, are just as adversely affected by the insanity of war as the soldiers themselves.

Spouses that are left behind are as emotionally traumatized as anyone when their soldier leaves them and they have no idea if their loved one is going to die. That uncertainty is very draining on a person's state of mind, not knowing if there will be any communication from their loved one or if they will ever hear from them alive again.

Imagine your child wondering why Mommy or Daddy is not there to tuck them into bed or read them a story at night. Imagine your son or your daughter ready for graduation day, and you not there to be a part of that once-in-a-lifetime moment.

So much has been taken from the people who have volunteered to fight wars in the name of defending this country, and the loss of their families can never be replaced. Anniversaries are missed, weddings of family members are missed, graduations, babyies' first steps, and countless other moments that most people who have never had to go to war take for granted.

I have attended memorial services for fallen soldiers from Fort Stewart, Georgia. I have seen and heard the grief of family members of the fallen soldiers, and it is a sound that I never want to hear again. It is so very senseless to me, and I was greatly affected by it. Imagine what those family members were feeling. The depth of their loss is immense, and I know that I don't have the words to say what I felt, much less to describe what the family members were feeling.

The grief felt by a mother, father, uncle or aunt, sister or brother, wife, or husband of someone whose life was taken by war cannot be lessened by the playing of "Taps" or receiving a folded flag. While they are customs offered out of respect, they are not a replacement for the life that has been taken so needlessly. So while we mourn our fallen comrades killed by the senseless violence that war is, let us not forget the families and the incredible loss and grief they have to suffer as well.

Sgt. Kevin Benderman,
Conscientious Objector to War

October 22, 2005
Veterans of the various wars this country has engaged in are not always treated with the same amount of honor and integrity they displayed during their term of service.

I have to ask, "Why is someone who is willing to put his or her life on the line for an ideal supposedly encouraged by the people of this country, treated like less than a valuable member of society upon their return from combat?" We expect our veterans to perform honorably under some of the most inhumane conditions during a war, and yet we believe they are less than honorable when they display the emotional and physical distress that comes from carrying out acts that are required under those difficult conditions. This current war is no different from others in that respect.

At Fort Stewart, Georgia, I was contacted by the mother of a young soldier who was destined to be released from the service due to a medical condition that caused neurological deafness. He held a medical report that labeled him as nondeployable, and was scheduled to face a hearing to be medically discharged. Rather than be placed in rear detachment to await this release, his first sergeant and another soldier entered his barracks room in the night, and ordered him to report for deployment to Iraq with his unit, or face eleven years in prison for desertion. This young soldier, not knowing that he had another option, is now serving in Iraq—hearing impaired.

Another soldier's family notified me that their loved one had been scheduled to be released from the service due to a partial paralysis in both arms. He had bone spurs on his cervical vertebrae pressing on his spinal cord that caused this condition, which was aggravated when he put on his Kevlar helmet. Even though he stood in formation, unable to raise his arms, and with his equipment on, unable to use his trigger finger due to the paralysis, this soldier's platoon sergeant threatened him with jail time for malingering, pretending injury to avoid serving his duty, and ordered him to deploy to Iraq.

Another young man from Fort Stewart, this soldier from the unit that I was in, attempted suicide as a result of severe PTSD, coming from his service during Operation Iraqi Freedom. This young soldier ingested 32 Percocet tablets in an attempted suicide and was admitted to the Liberty County Medical Center. When our company commander and battalion commander found out, they had him moved to the army hospital at Fort Stewart, where upon his arrival, the company commander accused him of malingering, and said he would stay in a hospital gown until five days later, when he would be deployed in handcuffs. The commanding officer restrained the soldier's wife from visiting him in the psych unit of the army hospital and berated her for assisting her husband. This soldier was ultimately ordered to deploy and receive his counseling treatment in a combat zone.

I ask you, is this the type of treatment soldiers deserve, especially from people who are in commanding positions in an organization for which they took an oath to protect their soldiers, no matter what?

I could list numerous other incidents such as these that I have witnessed in my ten years of service, but I believe you can get the gist of what I would like you to know just by hearing these three stories.

Veterans deserve better than this, regardless of what war they have had to fight. Veterans from past wars are now in danger of losing benefits, of being given less than honorable treatment for their service, and are being left forgotten while taxpayers' hard-earned money is going to finance an equally difficult war that is creating thousands of new veterans.

It is not about politics; it is not about ideologies. This battle for peace, in which I am now engaged, is about people, and sadly, the men and women who have put the most on the line for the people of this country are the ones being given the least respect by their fellow citizens now.

If Americans do not stand up and demand that they be represented with the integrity they deserve, it is not our country that will suffer—it is the people who make up this country that will lose.

Sgt. Kevin Benderman,
Conscientious Objector to War

October 22, 2005

"The buck stops here."

A simple statement that lets us know that responsibility for actions will not be shirked, or sent down to subordinates for blame. This statement was on a plaque on Harry S. Truman's desk while he served as president of our nation, and he employed that ideal in the daily undertaking of his duties.

I want to know what has happened to that philosophy of using integrity in the decisions made by our government, acting on them after careful thought to the consequences and accepting responsibility when the actions are wrong, even harmful to our country.

Everywhere you look today, you see finger-pointing, and people that we entrusted to hold offices in government with a certain level of integrity, acting like small children when they are up to mischief. This attitude has pervaded our highest levels of elected and appointed leadership positions.

This attitude of not taking responsibility for what has happened during their watch has reached appalling levels in this country. I believe that the reason for this condition is apathy, and the fact that it is so widespread throughout the citizenship of our nation. I don't know why we have become so apathetic as a people, but if we don't start caring soon, then the ideals of the founding fathers of this country are going to erode to the point where our nation will no longer stand. Our Constitution clearly gives the controlling power in this country to the American citizens. Unless the people of America wake up and take hold of the responsibility the Constitution ensures is their right, we will continue to see the decline of this country into a state where no one will be able to speak their mind or even exercise their basic rights.

We must not allow fear to dictate our actions, but we also must take action only after a well-thought-out plan is in place to be implemented to solve the problem. Roosevelt said that fear is all we have to be afraid of, but we are currently being told to be afraid of everything—even our shadows, it seems. Americans, it is past time to stand up, shake off our fear, and accept our responsibility.

"The buck stops here."

Sgt. Kevin Benderman,
Conscientious Objector to War

October 24, 2005
While I have been confined, I am still able to stay in touch with what is happening in our world. It has come to my attention that various groups around the country are planning on holding vigils upon the death of the 2,000th soldier in Iraq. I have also come to understand that there is almost a countdown to this event, as though this is something to look forward to—the death of a young man or woman to add clout to their cause. As a soldier, I can honestly say, I would not want

to hear that organizations were sending e-mails and planning the day of my death so that it may be used to further a political agenda under the guise of stopping the war, and giving their organization a more prominent platform.

Imagine what the young soldiers would think, or how they would feel, if they were to hear of such nonsense. I can tell you beyond a shadow of a doubt that no one is lining up to receive that distinction, so that they can become the poster child for the next effort to end the war. I have to personally say that this idea does not seem well thought out, if it has been thought through at all with regard to the feelings of the soldiers hearing what is being planned.

I also understand that there are people speaking of tying themselves to the fence outside of the White House in protest until all of the soldiers are returned home. Grandstanding such as this is not the way to get our troops home. All such stunts do is provide the proponents of this war fodder to prove that the antiwar crowd is just a bunch of half-baked ideologues with no sound solutions to the problem.

Instead of looking forward to the death of a service member or to grandstanding publicity stunts, why aren't we using all of this energy to create a well-organized approach to ending this war based on the facts surrounding the issues of the illegality of it? The Nuremberg Tribunal states that no country may take an aggressive military action against another unless it is an act of self-defense. The action taken against Iraq has now been shown clearly to not be one of self-defense, as stated by the findings of the 9/11 Commission. Iraq in no way attacked this country, nor was it aligned with Afghanistan. This particular provision of the Nuremberg Tribunal was introduced at the insistence of our government, and was signed by our president and ratified by our Congress as being legally binding upon the United States *forever*. It is this type of information that is going to have to be carefully interpreted, methodically developed, and presented in order to bring this madness to a halt. Grandstanding, providing no viable alternatives to the situation we now have, and using the death of the 2,000th American soldier to advertise a cause will not.

Sgt. Kevin Benderman,
Conscientious Objector to War

October 31, 2005
An Ounce of Prevention

How can we begin to resolve the issues that arise between the peoples of the world?

I don't proclaim to have all of the answers, but I believe a good way to start would be by utilizing sound foreign policy and a good application of diplomatic skills tempered with common sense. This combination could go a long way toward preventing a situation from escalating into the brutal stupidity of war.

When it comes to the indiscriminate death and destruction that comes from war, I believe the axiom "an ounce of prevention is worth a pound of cure," is the only way to approach the looming possibility. This leads to the question, "How can we prevent war in an increasingly unstable world?" This is a complex question for which there are no simple answers.

I believe that this country can help foster that "ounce of prevention" by no longer providing arms for unstable leaders, a statement supported by facts from the history of the development of our current situation. During the 1980s, when Iran was at war with Iraq, our elected leaders decided to assist Iraq by providing them with arms and training in military tactics. The study of our recent history verifies this through the facts. It goes to show that we helped create the atmosphere that got us bogged down in this current situation.

Another interesting fact is that Fort Leavenworth, Kansas, has a Command and General Staff College (CGSC). This college trains our officers in the tactics and techniques of war fighting. I was stationed at Fort Leavenworth from 1987 through 1991, and while there I witnessed Iraqi Army officers attending the CGSC in 1988. Imagine my surprise when we were going to war only two years later in 1990 in the Persian Gulf.

I suggest we stop arming and training the armies of governments that are not stable to begin with. Instead of military tactics and arms, I believe we should start exporting food production technology, medical technology, research and development on alternate fuel sources, or any other development programs that would benefit the collective needs of humanity.

To sum up, I certainly hope we all start practicing the "ounce of prevention" when it comes to the consideration of war, not only for our sake but for that of our children and grandchildren as well.

Sgt. Kevin Benderman,
Conscientious Objector to War

November 3, 2005

In order for us to eliminate war from our lives we are going to have to stop glorifying it in the eyes of our young people through the use of pop-cultural media, such as video games and movies. I have seen so many different movies and video games of this genre that I can't even count them all. Not one of these can even come close to the real horror of war. As a matter of fact, these video representations all seem to portray war as a tour filled with glamour and honor. Speaking from firsthand experience, I can honestly say that nothing could be further from the truth. War is the most inhumane and disgusting endeavor that mankind participates in. The modern weapons systems that are now assisting in our pursuit of annihilation of one another have to be seen in action in order to understand just how destructive to the human body they really are. Video games and movies cannot do this realistically.

It may seem clichéd, but war is moments of extremely tense waiting for shooting to start followed by long hours of monotonous and tedious activity designed to pass the time. After the initial adrenaline rush that comes when you cross the berm and you settle into the daily routine of existence in a war zone, you experience every emotion that humans possess and you see things that are able to sicken you to the core.

I cannot fully explain how I felt when I stood at the edge of a mass gravesite and saw the rotting bodies of women, children, and old men.

I can't explain the anger I felt when the equipment we took with us failed and caused a first lieutenant in my battalion to get killed.

No one can understand the anger I felt when the first sergeant gave orders that caused the soldiers I served with to be seriously injured for no good reason.

No one will ever know the anger that went through me when the company commander gave orders to shoot children when they were doing nothing more than tossing pebbles and laughing.

Let's stop glorifying this madness and show it for what it really is—Man's greatest inhumanity to Man.

Sgt. Kevin Benderman,
Conscientious Objector to War

November 5, 2005

We have witnessed the events unfold at the Abu Ghraib prison complex in Iraq. We have seen the destruction of hospitals and other civilian structures in the city of Fallujah. We have heard the reports of the bodies of dead combatants being set ablaze as a method of taunting the Al-Qaeda.

We hear our president calling for the torture of EPWs [enemy prisoners of war] and other combatants as a perfectly acceptable way of obtaining information, in spite of the fact that this country signed an international agreement to abide by the Geneva Conventions permanently.

We hear a senator calling for a reaffirmation to follow a higher path all the while this administration is attempting to drag us down to a level of government-authorized brutality never before practiced by the United States.

During World War II and the Holocaust against the Jewish nation, we were appalled at the treatment of human beings at the hands of a megalomaniacal politician, and yet it seems as though we are attempting to take a page out of a very disturbing period of history and incorporate it into our current life.

It seems that, if we are going to announce ourselves as a shining example for the rest of the world to emulate, then we had better ensure that we are above board in all of our actions, or else we are all just a bunch of hypocrites. I, for one, will never find these types of actions tolerable from my country, and I do not understand how a nation that claims to base itself upon the teachings of Christ can sit by idly while this happens.

Where is the moral outrage from our moral majority?

As our government calls repeatedly to make this type of mindless brutality legal, I have heard one voice in Congress calling for the rejections of such outright inhumanity. Are we going to add our voices to his to renounce this lunacy, or are we going to become willing accomplices in crimes against humanity?

Sgt. Kevin Benderman,
Conscientious Objector to War

November 5, 2005
Solutions to the situation we now face are very desperately needed. What can we do to solve the problem of war that is now in front of us? The first step, I think, is to start getting assistance from other Middle Eastern nations to help provide security for Iraq and training for their army. How do we accomplish this? The most important thing we have to do, as citizens of this country, is to inform our elected representatives that these types of solutions are what we want them to start working toward.

We are going to have to make them understand beyond a shadow of a doubt, this is the standard we expect them to meet. We must show them that we will not let them shirk their responsibility, by making a determined effort to hold them accountable for doing what is right in this current situation. This is a crucial step that must be taken in order to solve the problem we now find ourselves facing.

Once we get this immediate crisis under control, we, as American citizens, need to take a good, long look at ourselves and ask ourselves why we have become so apathetic and fearful of how our country is being run.

The U.S. Constitution gives us, the citizens, the ultimate responsibility for keeping this country running with the idea of doing what is right. For far too long we have given up that responsibility. We have allowed the employees of the United States to become our caretakers, and as a result, our elected representatives have become our quasi-parents.

I, for one, do not want my government to act as my parent or guardian. But I do expect them to perform the job they were hired to do within the guidelines of our Constitution.

There are certain individuals who are on the payroll currently, who feel that they are not governed by the laws of this nation. It is our duty, right, and responsibility to remind them of the fact that not one person is above the law. If we had continuously ensured that all of the laws were being followed, then this current situation would have never arisen in the first place. Now that it has, and if we truly believe it is the wrong direction for this country to be headed in, then stand up, call your hired employee, and inform them that we expect them to take the correct action, and come up with a viable plan to use to bring other countries on board to assist us in solving the problem that we have created in the Middle East.

In the future, we must not allow complacency and apathy to rule our actions. We cannot allow the atmosphere to grow where we expect our elected leaders to be our saviors or our parents that can solve all of our problems, paying no attention to their actions and neglecting to hold them accountable for the misguided ways in which they conduct our business.

Blind faith may be a viable condition of religion, but it will never work when it comes to politicians. We must actively take part in our government to ensure that we do not become involved in things that are not allowed by the laws established through the principles set forth in our Constitution.

Sgt. Kevin Benderman,
Conscientious Objector to War

November 6, 2005

When I decided to become a member of the Armed Forces of the United States, I took an oath to defend the Constitution and the ideals it set forth. In this document is a clause that states that any treaty that the United States enters becomes the Law of the Land. The Geneva Conventions is such a treaty. The United States, along with numerous other countries, worked to establish the principles of the Geneva Conventions, then agreed, in perpetuity, to abide by the laws that the conventions set forth with regard to the treatment of POWs.

During basic training all initial-entry soldiers are required to take a course covering the Geneva Conventions and the Law of Land

Warfare, which specifically prevents any service member from torturing or mistreating enemy prisoners of war in any way whatsoever. I learned to respect the fact that the professional soldiers of the United States were being instructed to perform their duties using a higher standard as being the only way to perform when dealing with captured enemy soldiers.

Upon reaching the rank of NCO serving this country, I was required to memorize the Noncommissioned Officer's Creed, which gives noncommissioned officers a strict outline of how you are to conduct yourself as an NCO in the U.S. military. One of the lines in the creed is, "I will never compromise my integrity nor my moral courage." After going to Iraq and seeing for myself that there were no WMDs present, and learning that we weren't really there to protect or liberate the Iraqi people, I realized that in order to follow the laws of this nation, and if I were to maintain my integrity, I could no longer take part in a war that at best was based on erroneous information. Now it is becoming more and more obvious that it was based on outright lies. With all of the information that continues to come out concerning the statements attempting to justify this crime against humanity, I made the decision to not compromise my integrity by filing for status as a conscientious objector to war. I decided to no longer participate in a war that was based on lies, which makes this war a crime against humanity, as defined by the Nuremberg Tribunal.

There was no other decision for me to make, as I would not have been able to look myself in the eye if I had returned to Iraq as a combatant in an illegal and immoral war.

Sgt. Kevin Benderman,
Conscientious Objector to War

November 16, 2005

Civilization or third world country? Democrats or Republicans? Conservative or liberal? Immigrants or native born? Old or young? Black or white? Labels, labels, labels. I have had it up to here with labels.

What will it take for people to realize that each and every one of us on the planet is human? As humans all of us have the same basic needs—food, shelter, and a desire to live in peace in our homes.

I want to know why we have allowed our differences to obscure our humanity. Across the world we have played up our differences to the degree that many nations spend large amounts of energy and resources developing vast arrays of weapons systems to destroy each other over differences in religious beliefs, cultural and political beliefs, and many other beliefs that do not justify the death and destruction that we have brought down on ourselves for far too long. How many more wars, deaths, and waste of our resources are we as humans going to tolerate before we realize that we are not reaping any positive benefits from what we have sown with the seeds of war and massive killings over the years?

We humans have killed millions of people throughout our centuries of existence and we continue to do so, all the while saying we are doing this to bring about peace. How colossally stupid a statement to make, and yet, many people actually believe that without war there would be no peace. People have actually made this statement to me with a depth of conviction that was rather alarming. The past century saw the most devastating, destructive force ever created unleashed on mankind with the event of the atomic bomb, and yet we still pursue the institution of war as though it were a viable way to solve our problems. I don't know about you, but I think that if the destruction of two cities and over two hundred thousand people with relatively small bombs is not enough to wake people up to the fact that our destructive capabilities are not the answer, then I don't have the slightest idea what will. But I sincerely think that we should start seriously reconsidering our approach to reconciling our differences because the policy of war is not the answer.

"Man must put an end to war, or war will put an end to mankind" (John F. Kennedy).

Sgt. Kevin Benderman,
Conscientious Objector to War

November 18, 2005
Recently I've heard quite a few stories about funding cuts for the VA, and I thought to myself, "Why would an administration that claims to be so concerned about the welfare of our service members allow these

cuts to be made?" And then I thought, "We should be ensuring that our veterans are given the same dedication to their long-term health care concerns as they brought with them to their tour of duty."

This current war is generating so many people with new demands for health care, both mental and physical, that it is incomprehensible to me that the VA budget would be cut. Especially in light of the fact that there are still thousands of veterans from the Persian Gulf War, Vietnam, Korea, and World War II that require and depend on the VA for health care.

Why are these VA cuts considered even remotely acceptable? The people who have served and worn the uniform of this country proudly are deserving of so much more than this type of disgraceful treatment. No veteran of combat from any of these wars should ever have to go to bed wondering if they are going to get the treatment they need and have earned at so great a cost to them. It enrages me to hear our government reneging on their end of the agreement made with our service members, who have kept up their end even as it cost them an arm or a leg.

Sgt. Kevin Benderman,
Conscientious Objector to War

November 22, 2005

Why has a group of people that deliberately misled not only Congress, but the American people as well, started showing signs of anger and extreme stress over the fact that these same American people are starting to realize the extent of just how badly they were misled?

The president is now running into locked doors in a desperate attempt to escape the truth. The vice president has resorted to saying that a 27-year veteran in the Marine Corps, who has received a Bronze Star and two Purple Hearts from action in Vietnam, has no spine and has mental failure. The president has started making remarks that members of Congress agreed with this illegal war based on the same intelligence he had.

I think we should examine this a little more closely in light of the Downing Street Memo, statements from Ambassador Joseph Wilson concerning the lack of evidence about Iraq's attempt to obtain enriched uranium, and various other sources that disprove this administration's claim that Iraq was involved in the September 11 attacks on our country, having plans to overthrow this country. How can the claim be made that Congress had the same information? All of these revelations came out after the war started, much later, and even after this information came out, this administration continued to attempt to discredit the people who provided the information. I have to ask, is this having the same access to enough pertinent information to declare a war? I don't think it is. Furthermore, I don't believe that members of Congress would make the same decision if they had access to the same intelligence the administration had.

Facts are there for anyone who wants to see them for themselves. The 911 Commission report states that although there was an attempt by Al-Qaeda to negotiate with Saddam Hussein to form an alliance, Hussein flatly refused to be associated with Al-Qaeda.

Facts show that Iraq did not attack the U.S. in any way whatsoever. This shows that what we did was launch an aggressive, preemptive war against a nation that had done nothing to provoke us into a self-defensive posture.

Facts will show that this is an illegal war as based on our laws. The Nuremberg Tribunal that came into existence after World War II as a result of Nazi aggression against neighboring countries specifically state that no nation can legally wage war against another unless it is for self-defense. The U.S., along with our Allies, contributed to drafting this document after the Nazi defeat to ensure that no one would ever again conduct preemptive military action against a sovereign nation. It was considered, agreed to, and signed into our laws in perpetuity by our Congress with no objection from any sector of our government. It is still in effect to this day.

Facts will show the conduct of this war to be illegal as well, as evidenced by the order of torture of enemy prisoners of war from the highest levels of the Department of Defense. Again, this nation's government considered and adopted the Geneva Conventions as a law of this nation in 1949, which have specific rules that outlaw torture of any type to any captured combatant. I qualify these statements, which prove these documents are the supreme law of the land, by highlighting our Constitution, which states that any treaty or other such documents agreed to by us, shall become the Supreme Law of the Land.

I respectfully but strongly urge all Americans to get copies of these documents and see for themselves what they contain. After studying them I have reached the conclusion that the initiation of the war was illegal and the conduct of parts of it is illegal as well. This has damaged America's credibility and our standing as a responsible world citizen.

I believe it is time for all Americans who hold true the ideals set forth by our Constitution to stand and be counted—not for what is politically expedient, but for what is morally right.

November 28, 2005

Kevin asked that I locate the words to this speech given by Franklin D. Roosevelt in 1936, his "I Hate War" speech, and post it in this blog as Kevin's statement for this week. For both of us, this speech says all that we could say about war and how it destroys. FDR is truly a man whose words should be respected, but sadly, we believe they have been forgotten.

In Peace,

Kevin and Monica Benderman

• • •

Franklin D. Roosevelt,
Chautauqua, New York

I Hate War

We are not isolationists except insofar as we seek to isolate ourselves completely from war. Yet we must remember that so long as war exists on earth there will be some danger that even the nation which most ardently desires peace may be drawn into war.

I have seen war. I have seen war on land and sea. I have seen blood running from the wounded. I have seen men coughing out their gassed lungs. I have seen the dead in the mud. I have seen cities destroyed. I have seen 200 limping, exhausted men come out of line—the survivors of a regiment of 1,000 that went forward 48 hours before. I have seen children starving. I have seen the agony of mothers and wives. I hate war.

I have passed unnumbered hours, I shall pass unnumbered hours thinking and planning how war may be kept from this nation.

I wish I could keep war from all nations, but that is beyond my power. I can at least make certain that no act of the United States helps to produce or to promote war. I can at least make clear that the conscience of America revolts against war and that any nation which provokes war forfeits the sympathy of the people of the United States. . . . The Congress of the United States has given me certain authority to provide safeguards of American neutrality in case of war. The President of the United States, who, under our Constitution, is vested with primary authority to conduct our international relations, thus has been given new weapons with which to maintain our neutrality.

Nevertheless—and I speak from a long experience—the effective maintenance of American neutrality depends today, as in the past, on the wisdom and determination of whoever at the moment occupy the offices of President and Secretary of State.

It is clear that our present policy and the measures passed by the Congress would, in the event of a war on some other continent, reduce war profits which would otherwise accrue to American citizens. Industrial and agricultural production for a war market may give immense fortunes to a few men; for the nation as a whole it produces disaster. It was the prospect of war profits that made our farmers in the west plow up prairie land that should never have been plowed but should have been left for grazing cattle. Today we are reaping the harvest of those war profits in the dust storms which have devastated those war-plowed areas.

It was the prospect of war profits that caused the extension of monopoly and unjustified expansion of industry and a price level so high that the normal relationship between debtor and creditor was destroyed.

Nevertheless, if war should break out again in another continent, let us not blink [at] the fact that we would find in this country thousands of Americans who, seeking immediate riches—fool's gold—would attempt to break down or evade our neutrality.

They would tell you—and, unfortunately, their views would get wide publicity—that if they could produce and ship this and that and the other article to belligerent nations the unemployed of America would all find work. They would tell you that if they could extend credit to warring nations that credit would be used in the United States to build homes and factories and pay our debts. They would tell you that America once more would capture the trade of the world.

It would be hard to resist that clamor. It would be hard for many Americans, I fear, to look beyond, to realize the inevitable penalties, the inevitable day of reckoning that comes from a false prosperity. To resist the clamor of that greed, if war should come, would require the unswerving support of all Americans who love peace.

If we face the choice of profits or peace, the Nation will answer—must answer—"we choose peace." It is the duty of all of us to encourage such a body of public opinion in this country that the answer will be clear and for all practical purposes unanimous. . . . We can keep out of war if those who watch and decide have a sufficiently detailed understanding of international affairs to make certain that the small decisions of each day do not lead toward war, and if, at the same time, they possess the courage to say "no" to those who selfishly or unwisely would let us go to war.

•   •   •

December 3, 2005

I am writing this to the people of America, with the hope that, if they feel they are being misled and misrepresented by this administration, they will urge their friends and family to contact their elected representatives in order to inform them that these types of actions are not the will of the American people.

The outrageous distortions of our constitutional laws being perpetrated as the facts, in an attempt to subjugate a sovereign nation in order to control that nation's mineral wealth makes me physically ill.

The real slap in the face is the fact that they are using our armed forces to do this under the guise of protecting us from terrorists. The audacity of these people, to play on the patriotism of our sons and daughters who proudly wear the uniform, is disgusting and beyond contempt in my book.

Designating the armed forces to achieve their personal goals of record profits for major oil corporations is the most underhanded and vile abuse of the trust our sons and daughters placed in the people that are behind this fiasco.

Even more so in light of the fact that the VA is currently cutting benefits of veterans even after those veterans have given an arm, a leg, or their mental and emotional health to fulfill the agreement they made out of a sense of duty, honor, and country.

When our sons and daughters are giving so much of themselves, and some of them are making the ultimate sacrifice, is it asking too much for these oil companies to sacrifice some of their profits?

Are these record profits being made to honor the sacrifice of our sons' and daughters' lives?

Or, are they being made off of their blood, sweat, and tears?

Is it really patriotism to stand by people that are breaking the laws of our nation, or are we just being manipulated by people who are concerned only with their personal agenda?

I will close this with a quote from Theodore Roosevelt: "Patriotism means to stand by the country; it does not mean to stand by the president or any other public official."

Sgt. Kevin Benderman,
Prisoner of Conscience,
Conscientious Objector to War

December 9, 2005
It has recently come to light that military personnel in Iraq are offering and publishing articles in newspapers and broadcasting news reports on the radio stations, and these actions are financed by the U.S. military through the Pentagon. While this appears to be a harmless

function of the U.S. military, designed to promote the positive aspects of the military involvement in everyday life of Iraqis, I believe that it leads to questions that should be answered in a cogent manner.

If we are on the right path, and we are doing the right thing for the Iraqi people, why do we have to publicly work to convince them of that fact?

Why do we feel it necessary to pay for these ads and broadcasts, and present them as impartial news from local outlets?

Where is the integrity in these types of actions? Why are the people responsible for this not being asked these questions in a straight-forward manner?

I met a lot of the Iraqi people during my six months in Iraq, and I didn't get the impression that they were a mindless group of helpless waifs that needed to be spoon-fed what to think about what they saw happening. You must understand, these people have not spent major portions of their lives in a Valium-induced stupor in order to cope with a very different set of circumstances the way we face challenges here in the U.S. We should not expect to have them react in the same way as we do when it comes to actions that are plain to see, as it seems they are able to see a bit more clearly. I see a pattern developing out of this administration and it is disturbing.

First, here in the U.S., we were told that the "big bad Saddam" had his hordes of crazed, bloodthirsty, maniacal Muslims at the shores of our country, each of them with an atomic bomb and WMDs. Now, certain elements of the military are going around telling Iraqi citizens just how great things are there; flowers are being planted by our soldiers, everyone is holding hands and singing "Kum-Ba-Yah," and it is getting to be a little bit of a stretch of the imagination. It is way past the time of the Truth needing to be told.

To quote Thomas Payne, "An army of principles can penetrate where an army of soldiers cannot."

Sgt. Kevin Benderman,
Conscientious Objector to War

December 11, 2005
The federal government has renewed the USA Patriot Act, and I personally believe that it is a sad day for America. The act purports to

make us safe from terrorists. But if we are fighting in the Middle East to keep them from coming here, why are we subjecting our own citizens to such police state tactics?

I think this act is designed to control Americans, to keep us from gaining any sense of organization and cooperation among ourselves. If we are suspicious of one another, then we are not paying attention to what some politicians are doing that is unethical or blatantly illegal.

Have we become such a nation of whiny, helpless, drug-ridden zombies that we are always looking for Big Brother to save us at the expense of our freedom and liberty? Patrick Henry, a genuine USA Patriot, said, "Give me liberty or give me death." Are we, as modern Americans, going to continue that call for Liberty, or are we going to pop a couple more Valiums and crawl back into bed?

I see little ribbons and signs everywhere saying, "We Support Our Troops." I think real support for our troops is for our citizens to bring some of the same amount of dedication to defending our Constitution through actions and not words, just as our soldiers have. Americans are going to have to stop expecting drugs and government to solve all of our problems.

Soldiers are going to need help from all citizens in defending our Constitution, as defending it requires much more than just going to war in some far-off land. It requires each and every one of us to first make sure that we have a good understanding of it, and then actively ensuring that the ideals of it are implemented into our every-day lives.

I don't think trying to escape from reality while we expect someone else to do all of our work for us is supporting our Constitution or our troops.

I know that through our history, there have been some dark moments, but where has the attitude of "I am going to stand on my own to get what I need" gone? Has all the Ritalin, Valium, and Prozac totally destroyed it? I sincerely hope it hasn't, for the sake of our future generations.

I will leave you with this quote from another genuine USA Patriot, Benjamin Franklin: "Those who would give up essential liberty for temporary safety deserve neither liberty nor safety."

Sgt. Kevin Benderman,
Conscientious Objector to War

December 26, 2005

We have been hearing many stories recently of the abuses of the eminent domain laws against citizens of America, in which corporations are stealing private property with the help of government agencies while this administration claims to be spreading freedom throughout the world.

We have been spreading democracy throughout the world for many years now, and yet it seems that we are continually losing our greater freedoms here in America through a slow process of attrition. Our government has concerned itself with the "freedom" of so many other nations that it has neglected ours here at home. In some cases, it has outright trampled on our citizens' freedoms purposely.

How can we claim to be the shining beacon of freedom from tyranny when our government allows and assists corporations to steal from us the very things that set us apart from totalitarian regimes—that is, our private property? This current guise is for local or state government to claim your property as condemned in order for developers to be able to offer you compensation for much less than the property is worth so that they are able to build condominiums or strip malls.

I ask you, America, is this the freedom imagined by the people who broke from England to found this country?

How can our nation's government tout freedom for everyone else in the world while it is so intent on crushing our freedoms with unlawful and unethical ideas, such as the current abuse of eminent domain, the USA "*Un*-Patriot Act," and by spying on Americans without warrants?

Americans, if you do not stand up to make your voice heard regarding such outrages as these, I fear freedom as we understand it is going into the dustbin of history, never to be had again. I am not looking forward to that—are you?

Sgt. Kevin Benderman,
Prisoner of Conscience,
Conscientious Objector to War

December 28, 2005

The FBI has been monitoring the homes, businesses, and mosques of Muslim communities throughout our nation with equipment designed to detect radiation. It has been accomplishing this while being parked in parking lots and on the streets near these various places. They are doing this under the guise of protecting us from terrorist attacks coming from elements of terror cells based in the U.S.

I personally believe this is going way over the line, as it seems to say that all Muslims could be suspected of plotting to wreak havoc in our country. To qualify this statement, let's go back to the bombing of the Federal Building in Oklahoma City that was carried out by Timothy McVeigh. Why didn't the government order the surveillance of all the homes, businesses, and churches of former military members or Caucasian Christians for sources of ammonia nitrate and fuel oil compound, which were used to blow up the Federal Building? Crazy, you say? Is it any more crazy than targeting all Middle Eastern Muslims?

We have got to get these knee-jerk reactions under control and start approaching this threat with a well-reasoned, thought-out plan. Acting like small children who jump at every shadow and bump in the night is not the way to protect ourselves from any type of threat or danger. Reacting out of fear always causes many more problems than it ever solves, and it is no different when it comes to our national security.

Sgt. Kevin Benderman,
Prisoner of Conscience,
Conscientious Objector to War

December 30, 2005

On 29 December 2005, NPR News reported on the situation in Iraq, and what they said was in stark contrast to what some people are trying to portray as a great foreign policy success for this administration. The three most alarming points of the story were Shiites and Sunnis are both claiming the entire election process was fraudulent as conducted, the electricity in Iraq is off five hours for every two hours it is on, and the U.S. is now getting 70% of the oil that Iraq is producing.

Whether or not you want to believe the facts, these are the results of our invasion and occupation of a country that had nothing to do with the 9/11 attack on our country.

We were lied to by an administration that is peopled by individuals who have stated their intent for world domination through the economic and military force of America.

At first, I bought this bill of goods, and went to that country thinking that I was doing what I had sworn to do—which was to defend America. But as I looked around and saw the lay of the land, I realized that I had been lied to, and that everyone in the military was being used and abused by a group of people who had only their interests at heart and did not care whose lives they destroyed to reach their goals.

So, on this thirtieth day of December, 2005, I hereby declare openly my objection to this travesty of justice and the abuse of our military members' patriotism.

I object to the needless deaths of nearly 2,200 servicemen and -women, the needless deaths of over 30,000 Iraqi citizens, countless wounded and psychologically traumatized men, women, and children as a result of these men abusing the authority they have been entrusted with.

I object conscientiously, morally, and ethically to these actions, which are an affront to my humanity, honor, and integrity as an American soldier, husband, and stepfather to three great young adults, man, and human being.

The United States Army decided to imprison me as a result of my recognizing the Truth and speaking out about it. I want the people responsible for that to know that I consider it an honor to be jailed for telling the Truth—far better than to be condemned to Hell for following a blatant lie that would result in my being an accomplice to such an atrocity.

Sgt. Kevin Benderman,
Conscientious Objector to War,
and the lies, corruption, and crimes against
humanity that must accompany it

July 5, 2006

When I was a young man, we were told to live in fear of the Communists. Now that I am a grown man, we are told to fear the terrorists. What will we be told to fear when I am an old man?

I am beginning to detect a pattern for how fear is used to strip away our freedoms. I think we need to be on the watch for all of these elements here in our very own country. Alarmists create the climate of fear whereby those in power are able to control your reactions to their manipulated stimulus. Absolute power does indeed corrupt absolutely.

I have reached a decision to no longer pay attention to all of the fear mongering from all of the Chicken Littles who have pervaded our government. I am going to put fear aside and look at the 21st-century challenges we face much more rationally.

If our nation is confronted with an unavoidable situation, then we should deal with it in a calm and rational manner in order to effect a well-thought-out and reasoned resolution.

In matters of national security, America does have every right to protect itself, but we should never endeavor to commit our military to defend against an imagined or blown-out-of-proportion threat.

If anyone in government abuses the commitment of the young men and women who have dedicated their lives to the defense of our way of life, that person should be held accountable for their actions, and if found guilty of any wrongdoing, prosecuted to the fullest extent of the law.

Americans are going to have to commit themselves to being proactive participants in our form of government. We all have the responsibility of ensuring that our government operates only within the guidelines and laws established by our Constitution. This is what Lincoln meant when he said that, "government of the people, by the people and for the people should not perish from the earth."

We cannot expect our government to do everything for us as we sit back and reap the rewards of others' labors. Each one of us has to actively contribute to our country by effectively participating in our government process.

We also need to remove the imaginary barriers that now exist between average Americans, erected by those who benefit from the divisions between the common people. America has not performed to her potential, and unless we bridge the gap that keeps us divided, America will not ever reach her potential. Americans, let's unite in our commonality so that we may better ourselves and our future generations instead of letting those who would benefit from the rift created by emphasizing our slight differences continue to tear us down.

The Rev. Martin Luther King Jr. had a dream that we all would sit down at the table of true brotherhood. I believe it is far past the time to make this dream a reality. Americans, there is a place for us all—won't you have a seat at the table?

Sgt. Kevin Benderman,
Prisoner of Conscience,
Conscientious Objector to War

July 20, 2006

Israel has declared all-out war against Lebanon and is currently in the process of attempting to bomb Beirut into oblivion.

Our current presidential administration seems to believe it is necessary to support this military action.

It is my firm opinion that we should not provide Israel with any military assistance or moral support as they continue to fight this unnecessary war.

As a matter of fact, Israel should realize the artificial creation of their state in 1948 is the root cause of their never-ending war since that time. Israel and NATO should have negotiated with the people that already had been long established in that region for the accommodation of the misplaced Holocaust survivors instead of bullying their way into an occupation.

The United States needs to stop aiding and abetting the long and extremely heinous cycle of war in this region and to begin to work with both sides to come up with a viable solution. If the two sides refuse to make any positive attempts to resolve this long-standing conflict, then we should no longer support either side.

As an average taxpayer, I'm tired of my tax dollars being spent on programs that allow this situation to continue to create instability in this region. If the nation of Israel wants to continue this madness, then let them do it on their own.

This never-ending war started in 1948, then simmered until 1967, then again until 1973, and has been going strong ever since. Nothing positive has been accomplished by all of this fighting, and for it to have continued this long is pure insanity.

For us to continue to support this madness through the sale of surplus military equipment and the training in the proper use of this equipment is a worthless waste of our time and resources. We have not benefited from this in any way.

As a matter of fact, our involvement in this situation has proven physically detrimental to our economy on at least one prior occasion, and it is apparently doing so again. The 1973 OPEC Oil Embargo against us was put in place because of our assistance to Israel. Now oil prices are close to $80 per barrel, which is having an extremely adverse effect on our economy.

For us to continue to throw good money after bad in this situation makes absolutely no sense. It is far past the time for Israel to wean itself from the American teats and to reach a sound compromise in the region, or get out.

Either way, the United States should stop assisting Israel, and start giving the resources we have wasted on this insanity to reduce our national deficits and to resolve other problems we face here at home.

Sgt. Kevin Benderman,
Prisoner of Conscience,
Conscientious Objector to War

July 20, 2006

There seems to be a large consensus among people who want to stop war that the best way to accomplish this is to urge soldiers, sailors, marines, and airmen to just up and leave their post. This is an unrealistic and irresponsible viewpoint that is unattainable.

Turn the issue around. What would you do if a service member told you to quit your job, stop paying taxes, and run to Canada or Mexico in order to take away finances and possible personnel used to fight the war? "Unrealistic," you may say, and you would be correct in that assessment. It is just as unrealistic for anyone to expect service members to just walk away from what they have invested so much of themselves in.

If you want to "support our troops" as much as you say, then stop putting all the responsibility on them with the unrealistic expectation for them to just quit. What we need to do as a group of well-organized, concerned citizens is to set down a clear plan for how we want to accomplish our goals and then implement that plan. Dragging out all the old, worn-out, and ineffective methods used during the '60s to protest isn't going to work. It didn't work then and it isn't going to work now.

What will work is to get a copy of our Constitution, familiarize ourselves with it, and understand what its laws mean. What will work is for citizens of this country to learn their responsibility to this country and to honor it with more than words on signs.

We must realize that our efforts should be directed toward reaching a consensus among ourselves about how we want to accomplish our goals in order to provide for mortgage payments, truck and car payments, child care, and all other living expenses our soldiers are responsible for before you boldly continue with public statements encouraging our young service members to simply walk or run away.

So put down your picket signs, go home, get familiar with the documents that govern our laws, organize your community groups of conscientious citizens willing to communicate with their elected representatives, and work with them to reach a positive solution to the adverse action now affecting all of us. It is your responsibility to be actively involved with our government officials to see that the laws of our nation ethically and morally represent the principles of our Constitution, and this will not be accomplished by yelling in the streets. It will be accomplished by people coming together, hearing all sides, and realizing that compromise is needed in order to achieve results that fairly represent the rights of all people in this country.

"Supporting the troops" is not flag waving; it is not attaching yellow, purple, or red-white-and-blue plastic ribbons to our gas tanks, and it is not waving signs in the streets. There is no support for the troops when people encourage them to simply quit their posts while those same people are refusing to take an active role in seeing that there is something positive in place for those "troops" to report to.

It is the responsibility of all United States citizens to see that our laws are protected from the abuse of unscrupulous individuals who seek power for their own gain, and this is accomplished through active participation, not cheerleading from the streets.

Sgt. Kevin Benderman,
Prisoner of Conscience,
Conscientious Objector to War